Life-Changing Spiritual Practices
Volume 1

*Individual spiritual practices to build into your lifestyle,
as you walk the spiritual path on practical feet*

Rev. Bil Holton, Ph.D.
Rev. Cher Holton, Ph.D.
YourSpiritualPractice.com

Copyright ©2015 Bil Holton and Cher Holton

All rights reserved.

Reproduction or translation of any part of this work beyond that permitted by Section 107 or 108 of the 1976 United States Copyright Act without the permission of the copyright owner is unlawful. Requests for permission or further information should be addressed to the authors, c/o Prosperity Publishing House, 1405 Autumn Ridge Drive, Durham, NC 27712.

This publication is designed to provide accurate and authoritative information in regard to the subject matter covered. It is sold with the understanding that the publisher is not engaged in rendering legal, accounting, clinical counseling, or other related professional service. If legal advice or other expert assistance is required, the services of a competent professional person should be sought. From a Declaration of Principles jointly adopted by a Committee of the American Bar Association and a Committee of Publishers.

Prosperity Publishing House
Durham, NC

Library of Congress Cataloging-in-Publication Data

Holton, Bil
Making Your Life a Spiritual Practice, Volume 1 / Bil Holton and Cher Holton
      p. cm.
  Includes bibliographical references.
  ISBN 978-1-893095-90-8
  1. Spiritual   2. New Thought   3. Self Help
  II. Title

Library of Congress Control Number: 2015943622

Printed in the United States of America

10 9 8 7 6 5 4 3 2 1

To the Divine within you

***Photo Credits, used with permission:*成**

Cover Design: © Cher Holton
Page 5: © 2015 clipart.com
Page 6: © Jochenschneider | Dreamstime.com
Page 7: © Celia Maria Ribeiro Ascenso | Dreamstime.com
Page 9: © Lammeyer | Dreamstime.com
Page 11: © Cher Holton
Page 12: © 2015 graphicstock.com
Page 13: © 2015 clipart.com
Page 14: © Cher Holton
Page 18: © Cher Holton
Page 19: © 2015 clipart.com
Page 20: © 2015 clipart.com, modified by Cher Holton
Page 21: © 2015 clipart.com
Page 22: © 2015 clipart.com, modified by Cher Holton
Page 24: © 2015 clipart.com
Page 25: © Cher Holton
Page 28: © 2014 gaillynphotography.com
Page 29: © 2015 clipart.com, modified by Cher Holton
Page 31: © 2015 clipart.com
Page 32: © 2015 clipart.com
Page 33: © 2015 clipart.com
Page 34: © Joy Prescott | Dreamstime.com
Page 35: © 2015 clipart.com
Page 36: © 2015 clipart.com
Page 38: © 2015 graphicstock.com
Page 39: © 2015 graphicstock.com
Page 40: © 2015 iStock.com
Page 41: © 2015 clipart.com
Page 42: © 2015 graphicstock.com
Page 45: © 2015 clipart.com
Page 46: © 2015 clipart.com
Page 47: © stockXchange.com 972527_55259877
Page 48: © 2015 clipart.com
Page 49: © Cher Holton
Page 50: © Madmaxer | Dreamstime.com

Page 51: © 2015 clipart.com
Page 53: © 2015 clipart.com, modified by Cher Holton
Page 54: © 2015 clipart.com
Page 55: © Guillermain | Dreamstime.com
Page 56: © 2015 clipart.com
Page 57: © Wiscan | Dreamstime.com
Page 58: © 2015 graphicstock.com
Page 59: © Anpet2000 | Dreamstime.com
Page 60: © 2015 graphicstock.com
Page 61: © Cher Holton
Page 62: © graphicstock.com
Page 63: © 2015 clipart.com
Page 65: © graphicstock.com
Page 67: © 2015 clipart.com.com
Page 69: © TMarchev | Dreamstime.com
Page 70: © Cher Holton
Page 71: © Cher Holton
Page 73: © clipart.com
Page 75: © Cher Holton
Page 76: © graphicstock.com, modified by Cher Holton
Page 77: © 2015 cliparte.com
Page 78: © 2015 clipart.com
Page 79: © Cher Holton
Page 80: © Vladyslav Starozhylor | Dreamstime.com
Page 81: © Jacoboanastas | Dreamstime.com
Page 82: © ThreeriversII | Dreamstime.com
Page 83: © Cher Holton
Page 84: © Koolander | Dreamstime.com
Page 85: © sergeypeterman | Dreamstime.com
Page 86: © 2015 clipart.com
Page 87: © Rudall30 | Dreamstime.com
Page 89: © 2015 clipart.com
Page 90: © Leigh Prather | Drcamstime.com
Page 91: © Dawn Hudson | Dreamstime.com
Page 92: © Amnetorp | Dreamstime.com
Page 93: © Cher Holton
Page 94: © Cher Holton
Page 95: © graphicstock.com
Page 96: © 2015 clipart.com
Page 97: © 2015 clipart.com
Page 98: © 2015 clipart.com
Page 99: © Gbruer | Dreamstime.com
Page 100: © 2015 clipart.com
Page 101: © 2015 gaillynphotography.com

Table of Contents

Introduction	1
Abracadabra-ing	5
Vocal Acupuncture	6
Random Acts of Kindness	7
Aging Gracefully	9
Affirmations: Sell Yourself on Yourself	10
Ananda Moments	12
Ambitious Carding	13
12 Powers Centering Experience	14
Be Kind to Animals	18
Backpacking	19
Draft a Truth Seeker Bill of Rights	20
Book Study	21
Breathing Space	22
Burning Bowl	23
Be Your Personal Change Master	25
Refrain From Cell Phone Saluting	28
Get Clear About Crossing Over	29
Celebrate Small Wins	31
Chanting / Reciting Mantras	32
Communing With Nature	33
Consult Your Crystal Ball	35
Your Daily Red and Bread	36
Dancing	38
Routine Daily Activities	39
Defriending Dogma	40
Drawing / Painting	41
An In-Depth Reading: Fasting From Error	42
Footprints in the Sand (Our Version)*	47
Repair Rocky Roads With Forgiveness	48
Gardening / Landscaping	49
Googling, Yahooing, Binging	50
Grailology	51
Cultivate an Attitude of Gratitude	53
Eliminating Harmaceuticals	54
Hobbies / Crafts	55
Horseback Riding	56
iPad-ing	57

Jogging	58
Keurig Moments	59
Letting the Real You Out	60
Conduct a Language Audit	62
Laughing For Laughter's Sake	63
Soulful Music	65
Multiple Listings	66
Omvana	69
An In-Depth Reading: Don't Suffer From a Pain in the Ask	71
Rendezvous With Your Past, Present and Future	76
Peace Vigil	77
Enjoying the Performing Arts	78
Philanthropy	79
Still Photography	80
Time Lapse Photography	81
A Penny for Your Positive Thoughts	82
Pinteresting	84
Sacred Reading and Study	85
Eliminating Religious Relics	86
Take a 'Self to Cell' Journey	87
Silent Relaxation	89
Smartphoning	90
Create a Sound Byte Directory	91
T'ai Chi Movement	92
Resolute Thingumajiging	93
Honor Your BS	94
Take 365 Vacations	95
Volunteering	96
An In-Depth Reading: Work All Things Together For Good	97
YouTubing	99
Yoga Practice	100
About the Authors	101

Introduction

Spiritual practice refers to the intentional and purposeful choices you make, actions you take, soul deepening habits you adopt, and rituals you perform each day to nurture your connection with your Divine Nature. It means becoming consciously one with the Eternal Presence within expressing as your Higher Self, so you can master the art of living by staying connected with your own truth and purpose.

It is an intentional personal journey inward to experience your 'soul-fulness.' And you do that by building into each day spiritual practices that keep you focused on your spiritual growth. A spiritual practice is not a dogmatic path, nor is it a 'worship a god in the sky who is an entity separate from you' path. It is a path of Self-realization that acknowledges you are the human expression of the Eternal Presence (God) expressing Itself at the point of you.

Spiritual practices can take many forms. And that's the wonderful thing about devoting yourself to a spiritual practice. You can decide what practices constitute your over-all practice! While the forms of spiritual practices may differ, the intent is the same: nurturing the connection with your Higher Self which we call the Extraordinary You.

> *We need to make the conscious awareness of our divinity a habit. The more we live in that consciousness, the better our chances will be to master our human experience.*
> *(Bil & Cher Holton)*

The spiritual practices we share in Volume 1 are all sacred experiences, whether they involve just a few precious moments or take longer nuggets of your time. Developing a regular spiritual practice is a highly personal and intuitive process. We feel certain you'll find the perrrr-fect practices that resonate with your core being.

We applaud your desire to live a more spiritual life. You'll find it's the difference between surviving and thriving. The transformation you're seeking—we're all searching for—is possible when we enrich and enliven our lives by adopting a daily spiritual practice.

Choose what works for you. Adopting a practice someone else recommends is not nearly as important as how you *feeeel* while you're engaged in it. Be willing to "try out" a number of these practices. Look for a good fit between the practice and you. When you commit to a practice, see it as one of the ways to express your spiritual unfoldment. Make it high on your lifestyle priority list. See it as concrete evidence of walking your talk.

Spiritual Practices

Abracadabra-ing

This spiritual practice employs mindfulness meditation, affirmative prayer, visualization, and positive affirmations as the open sesames to healing and enlightenment. Abracadabra, as an incantation, was first used in the third century AD in a book called *Liber Medicinalis* by Sammonicus, a Roman savant and physician.

He recommended wearing an amulet displaying the word written in the form of a triangle:

```
A - B - R - A - C - A - D - A - B - R - A
A - B - R - A - C - A - D - A - B - R
A - B - R - A - C - A - D - A - B
A - B - R - A - C - A - D - A
A - B - R - A - C - A - D
A - B - R - A - C - A
A - B - R - A - C
A - B - R - A
A - B - R
A - B
A
```

The power of the amulet was believed to cure diseases and guarantee health and longevity. **From a spiritual perspective, it is the 'abracadabra nature' of the divinely ordained powers within us—and not an external physical object like an amulet—that cure illnesses and disease, and guarantee us the health, wealth, and happiness we seek!**

Here's How This Spiritual Practice Works:

This powerful spiritual practice invites you to employ all of the practices mentioned in the opening paragraph as spiritual 'amulets.' Spend time in the Silence, affirm your connection with Spirit, visualize your alignment with your Higher Self, and repeat positive statements about your intentions to be, do, and have from a consciousness of abundance, gratitude and connection.

© 2014 Bil and Cher Holton, YourSpiritualPractice.com

Vocal Acupuncture

The more well-known form of acupuncture which everyone is familiar with is an alternative healing technique based on traditional Chinese medicine. It involves the penetration by single-use thin needles along the skin of the body, or the application of heat, pressure, or laser light to correct imbalances in the flow of qi through channels in our bodies called meridians.

Vocal Acupuncture is the name we use to describe the power of spoken affirmations. Psychologist Barbara Fredrickson assures us that people who experience more positivity and then voice it become "more optimistic, more resilient, more open, more accepting, and more purpose-driven." She goes on to say that "positivity opens your mind and allows you to appreciate what is in such a way that you want to talk about it, which reinforces your positive outlook."

In his bestselling book, *Buddha's Brain*, Rick Hanson says, "Every time you say a positive affirmation, every time you engage in positive self-talk, every time you sift positive feelings and views into painful, limiting states of mind—you build new neural structures. Over time, the accumulating impact of this positive material will, synapse by synapse, change your brain in positive, life-affirming ways."

Neuroscientists are telling us that certain positive words—like 'peace,' 'compassion,' 'joy,' 'kindness,' and 'love'—have the power to alter the expression of genes throughout the brain and body, turning them on and off in ways that lower physical and emotional stress.

According to positive psychologists Rowe, Hirsch, and Anderson, another practical consequence of positivity's mind-broadening powers is enhanced creativity. A broad mindset changes the way you think and act in a wider range of circumstances. When you see more, more ideas come to mind, more actions become possible.

Here's How This Spiritual Practice Works:

As you can see, this spiritual practice offers you mental, emotional, physical, and spiritual health. Positiveness, in all of its forms and expressions, is a centering practice, one that increases your chances of walking the spiritual path on practical, positive feet. As a spiritual practice, Vocal Acupuncture invites you to use positive affirmations; affirmative prayer; mantras, optimistic phrases, and positive self-talk as often as you can. It means intentionally building these positivity statements into your spoken words and vocabulary.

© 2013 Bil and Cher Holton, YourSpiritualPractice.com

Random Acts of Kindness

Practicing random acts of kindness is a deliberate attempt to brighten another person's day by doing something thoughtful, nice, and heartfelt. Kindness is a way of showing others that they count. It is a spiritual practice that sends the message that generosity, kindness, and compassion are the kind of virtues that define a healthy society.

By practicing kind acts toward others, you're helping to create a kindness-aware climate that fosters communities that value generosity of spirit and action. In a study published in an online edition of the Proceedings of the National Academy of Sciences, researchers have provided evidence that cooperative behavior is contagious. When people receive kindness they tend to "pay kindness forward" by showing kindness to others. This cascade of kindness and generosity spreads, creating a multiplier effect. Each act of kindness is like a "matching grant" of (reciprocal) kindness that is truly contagious (James Fowler and Nicholas Christakis, "Connected: The surprising power of our social networks and how they shape our lives," Proceedings of the National Academy of Sciences, 107(9) 5334 – 5338, March, 2010).

There are many ways of practicing kindness, of which these are just a few:
- Cook a healthy meal for someone,
- clean a friend's house,
- give some change to another customer to help pay for his/her purchase,
- thank your bus or taxi driver,
- deliver a dessert to firefighters and/or school teachers,
- help a child start a piggy bank,
- help someone find a job,
- mow a senior citizen's lawn,
- pay someone's parking meter before it expires,
- leave Post-it Notes with inspirational messages on them for colleagues to see.

Since we're sowing acts of kindness, here are a few more:
- send someone an eCard,
- spend time with someone who needs someone who will listen,
- buy someone a book,
- write a positive blog post,
- praise someone,
- give a homeless person something to wear,
- show compassion to someone you may dislike,
- send notes of appreciation,

Life-Changing Spiritual Practices, Volume 1

- give money to down and out people on the side of the road,
- be generous with compliments,
- say 'Bless you' when someone sneezes,
- post inspirational quotes on your Facebook, Pinterest, Instagram, and other social media pages,
- help someone financially,
- pet-sit for someone,
- email a quick note to a friend who needs to 'hear' a kind word,
- let someone go in line in front of you,
- take a photo of people who want to capture a vacation moment together,
- wash someone's car,
- give theatre tickets away for free,
- shovel snow for a neighbor,
- tip big for extraordinary customer service,
- treat a friend to some fresh fruit,
- politely let another driver merge in front of you,
- call a friend who is sick,
- give a napkin folded into a rose to a waitress for her excellent service.

Practicing random acts of kindness is a spiritual practice that is congruent with the very concept of practicing spirituality itself.

Here's How This Spiritual Practice Works:

Each day, look for five opportunities to "pay kindness forward"—and notice the impact it has on your own well-being! Email us to let us know what you did … and/or what you discovered about the effect on you!

© 2003, 2010 Bil and Cher Holton, YourSpiritualPractice.com

Aging Gracefully

Aging gracefully is possible no matter who you are or what kind of life experiences you have had getting to where you are today. The process of growing older is a natural process for all of us. Grappling with the illnesses and deaths of parents and friends; the sudden transitions of family members and friends younger than us; age-related physical limitations; loss of flexibility, mobility and vigor are all representative of the aging process.

However, aging as a spiritual practice is not about diet, exercise, medications, bingo, crossword puzzles, or memory exercises. Why? Because aging can also be characterized by a zest for life, health and fitness, optimism and positivity, travel, cultivating meaningful relationships, spiritual growth, meaningful work, learning new talents and skills, new beginnings and fresh insights, and redefining what aging is all about.

Aging as a spiritual practice sees our later years not as a time of decline, but as a time of fulfillment and completeness as spiritual beings who are getting near the end of our earth experience. Preparing ourselves for mastering the art of living starts with cultivating our inner life, acknowledging our dynamic relationship with our Higher Self, and striving to align our human self with our Higher Nature.

Take a peek at Lewis Richmond's book, *Aging as a Spiritual Practice*. It'll help alleviate any doubts you may have about aging gracefully. Aging well starts where you are now. It's never too late (or too early) to start a spiritual practice that brings you into the wholeness and happiness you deserve.

Here's How This Spiritual Practice Works:

Spend time reflecting on yourself, and how you feel about the aging process. Write down all the positive aspects of aging, and what you love about the age you are now. Set an intention of focusing on the benefits of your aging process, and commit to doing one thing every day that celebrates you!

© 2009, 2014 Bil and Cher Holton, YourSpiritualPractice.com

Affirmations: Sell Yourself on Yourself

Do you talk to yourself? Do you talk to yourself out loud? Now for the totally revealing question: Do you answer yourself? (We believe those who answer affirmatively are the truly sane people ... they definitely know a good conversationalist when they find one).

Seriously, research says we all talk to ourselves—and 75-95% of what we say is usually negative. Take a few moments to consider how you talk to yourself. Have you ever leveled criticism at yourself?

If you have used self-demeaning comments to describe yourself, it's time to re-program your messages. **What you tell yourself has a direct relationship on your ability to handle stress; deal with people; achieve personal, professional, and spiritual goals; and connect with your Higher Self.** We unabashedly advocate selling yourself on yourself.

Here's How This Spiritual Practice Works:

Develop a set of short, powerful, positive affirmations about yourself. We call them Personal Empowerment Triggers (aka, PET phrases). Here are a few examples:
- I am one with the Inexhaustible Source of my abundant supply and I am blessed with awesome prosperity.
- I am one with the Eternal Presence and I have such heir power that I attract and enjoy unlimited abundance.
- Because I am one with my Higher Self, I enjoy peace, health, and plenty in all areas of my life.
- I am one with Infinite Intelligence and I live joyfully and prosperously at the speed of my Christ Consciousness.

We invite you to create PET's of your own. Two rules are in order as you prepare your PETs:
- Keep your PETs positive and life-affirming. Instead of saying things like, "I am no longer tired," say, "I am filled with vibrant energy."
- Keep PETs in the present tense. Avoid phrases like: *I'm going to be able to speak in public with confidence someday. I intend to be more successful at living the truth principles I know.* Instead, give yourself positive launches like: *I speak in front of groups with ease and confidence. I am living the truth principles I know joyfully and successfully everyday.*

Develop two types of PETs. One set includes a **core curriculum**: PETs that are related to your general attitude, philosophy, and well-being (*I am rich, well, and happy in all areas of my life*). The other type relates to specific spiritual goals (*I live a Christ-centered life. I am aligning my human self with my SuperSelf™, my True Self, with speed, ease, comfort, and joy*).

Take a few minutes to either write a couple of PETs or retrieve a few of your favorite affirmations. You may even want to modify them based on the "rules" we've shared. (Go ahead and take care of that. We'll wait)!

Now, review them quickly and then affirm each of them aloud several times.

How did it feel to write, modify, find your PETs? Most people admit that after the initial awkwardness of saying positive things about themselves disappears, this activity feels pretty good.

Record your PETs as a message to yourself on your smart phone or on a CD—or even videotape yourself. Be as up-beat and enthusiastic as possible. Then, on your way to and from work or when you're running errands, call up your message on your smart phone or pop the CD into your CD player. Reinforce your success with your own personalized sell yourself on yourself pep talk.

Don't feel frustrated if you don't believe yourself initially. When you get serious about something, self-doubt tends to creep in just a little. After all, you have accumulated a lifetime of negative self-talk. ***The important thing to remember about affirmations is that you're not saying affirmations to make them true, you're affirming them because they are Truth.***

© 2001, 2009 Bil and Cher Holton, YourSpiritualPractice.com

Ananda Moments

The word *Ananda* means 'bliss' in Pali and Sanskrit, as well as in other Indian languages. So, this spiritual practice advocates moments of joy, happiness, and bliss as we connect with our SuperSelf™ (Higher Self, Christ Self, God, the Eternal Presence). To achieve a state of extreme happiness, ecstasy and completeness is the essence of this practice.

A state of bliss results from being unified with the Universe through your super-consciousness. When you reach a blissful state, there is a deep knowing that you are one with all things, and that oneness is at the core of who you are.

Blissfulness gives you a moment-to-moment spiritual experience that is opening, trusting, and softening into each new moment of your life. Samādhi is a state of transcendental bliss. It is the eternally expanding realization that your ego is not real, and that you (the soul, spirit, and divine essence) are what is truly real and will never die. Samādhi is a Sanskrit term used in Hinduism, Buddhism, Jainism, and Sikhism that refers to a higher level of concentrated meditation. It is a non-dualistic state of consciousness in which the consciousness of the experiencing subject (the meditator) becomes consciously one with the experienced object (the Eternal Presence, God).

Here's How This Spiritual Practice Works:

This spiritual practice encourages you to set a daily intention of experiencing moments of extreme happiness, ecstasy, and joy. They may occur from meditation experiences, becoming totally absorbed in a sunset or star-studded sky at night, being immersed in a physical and/or mental activity that brings you incredible joy, or experiencing heart-melting music—to name a only a few.

© 2014 Bil and Cher Holton, YourSpiritualPractice.com

Ambitious Carding

For magicians, an ambitious card is a card effect where a selected card continually rises to the top of the deck after being placed into the middle of the deck. You've probably seen the trick and wondered how the slight-of-hand works. (The magicians aren't telling!)

From a spiritual perspective, Ambitious Carding is the psychosomatic process where a particular truth principle surfaces into your conscious awareness to help center you when you face life challenges, disappointments, and setbacks. It is a good spiritual practice to adopt because it helps you stay positive and optimistic.

What makes ambitious carding work as a spiritual practice is the amount of time you spend in esoteric and metaphysical study. The more you immerse yourself in higher thought, the greater your chances are in 'calling up' the learning. The more spiritual principles and teachings you know and use, the more these teachings will rub off on you. You'll have favorite teachings, be attracted to life-changing concepts, and remember maxims that have changed you at a soul level.

Here's How This Spiritual Practice Works:

Make the following statement a non-negotiable habit: "Every time I face a troublesome life situation I'm going to say to myself '*What spiritual principle can I use to give me the wherewithal to handle this situation?*'"

It sounds so simple, but it works. Having the intention to purposefully call upon the spiritual principles you know is a prerequisite for drawing them from your memory banks and making recall easier. It's just like that magician's ambitious card!

These instant reminders are what keeps you on your spiritual path instead of wandering off into the barbs and briars of stray paths. It almost feels like magic!

© 2014 Bil and Cher Holton, YourSpiritualPractice.com

Life-Changing Spiritual Practices, Volume 1

12 Powers Centering Experience

This is an extremely powerful guided meditation, based on the 12 Powers or Spiritual abilities we all have within us. (If you want to learn more about the 12 Powers, we recommend a great book—okay, full disclosure, we co-authored it—entitled *Power Up Your Life: Accessing Your Twelve Powers to Achieve Health, Happiness, Abundance, and Inner Peace*—ISBN 978-1-893095-84-7).

Here's How This Spiritual Practice Works:

Record this meditation on a CD so you can sit quietly and enjoy your experience. *Note: Wherever you see three dots, it indicates a pause so you can be totally immersed in the image being invoked.*

Once it is recorded, set aside a minimum of 30 minutes, and find a quiet place where you can sit comfortably and move through the meditation.

When the recording has completed, remain quietly peaceful for 5-10 more minutes, absorbing the rich benefits of what you have experienced. We also recommend journaling about your experience, capturing feelings, thoughts, and images you received throughout the meditation.

This is one that can be revisited often!

Here's the Script:

Take a nice, deep breath, and follow it as it moves throughout your body. ...

Again, take another breath -- inhale slowly ... exhale slowly. And again, allowing awareness to move gently from head to heart ...

Imagine a light glowing from deep within your being. As you continue to focus on this light, it grows ... and begins to flood your entire body ... carrying beautiful light to every cell and atom, every muscle, every fiber of your being. Take a moment and embrace the knowing that you are a glowing beautiful body of light. ...

Now, imagine that light becoming a beautiful royal blue color. ... This is your Power of FAITH, shining at its highest, most elevated level. FAITH is filling you with the Power to spiritually know and trust absolutely. With FAITH, you believe with confidence and conviction all the Spiritual Truths ...

Take in this affirmation: I claim FAITH now. Today, I refuse to allow doubt or fear to have a space in my consciousness. I stand firmly in FAITH and do what is mine to do. ...

As you continue focusing on the light radiating from within you, it now becomes a beautiful spring green color. ... This is your Power of STRENGTH, shining at its highest, most elevated level. Divine STRENGTH brings you the Power to stay the course and persevere. With STRENGTH, you are resilient ... and mentally tough in the midst of difficult circumstances. You can move through difficulties, knowing you have this Power within you. ...

Take in this affirmation: I claim STRENGTH now. Today, I will not give up or give in! I stand firm in STRENGTH and stay the course to achieve results. I am resilient; I am strong. ...

As you continue focusing on the light radiating from within you, it now becomes a beautiful shade of pink. ... This is your Power of LOVE, shining at its highest, most elevated level. Divine LOVE brings you the Power to harmonize and unify. With LOVE, you see the good and the best in everyone and everything, and love yourself and others unconditionally. ...

Take in this affirmation: I claim LOVE now. Today, I see the world through the eyes of LOVE. I choose to bring harmony to every situation, and I behold the highest and best in myself and in everyone I meet. ...

As you continue focusing on the light radiating from within you, it now becomes a vivid purple color. ... This is represents POWER, shining at its highest, most elevated level. Divine POWER allows you to claim dominion and mastery over the world of appearance, and bring ideas into manifestation with your word. ...

Take in this affirmation: I claim POWER now. Today, I will not be fooled by the world of appearance. I will only make statements I want to see manifest in my reality. I choose to use POWER to put the spiritual Truth principles into action so I can master the art of living. ...

As you continue focusing on the light radiating from within you, it now becomes a soft, glowing light blue. ... This is your Power of IMAGINATION, shining at its highest, most elevated level. Divine IMAGINATION brings you the Power to visualize and think outside the box. With IMAGINATION, you can claim a multitude of Divine Ideas and imagine being the best you can be. ...

Take in this affirmation: I claim IMAGINATION now. Today, I see incredible opportunities everywhere. I think way outside the box, and recognize solutions to everything I thought was a problem, as I use IMAGINATION to discover new horizons. ...

As you continue focusing on the light radiating from within you, it now transforms into a brilliant gold color. ... This is your Power of UNDERSTANDING, shining at its highest, most elevated level. Divine UNDERSTANDING brings you the Power to comprehend all things ... With UNDERSTANDING, you listen to your Intuition, and are able to make deep cognitive connections as you move beyond mere knowledge and grasp the deeper Truths. ...

Take in this affirmation: I claim UNDERSTANDING now. Today, I make time to spend in the Silence, and I know that I know that I know. Through UNDERSTANDING I am able to make the connections and experience the power of true knowing. ...

As you continue focusing on the light radiating from within you, it now shifts into a beautiful, soft and glowing color of yellow. ... This is your Power of WISDOM, shining at its highest, most elevated level. Divine WISDOM brings you the Power to apply what you know and understand. With WISDOM, you are able to discern what is in alignment with Truth and know how to move forward. ...

Take in this affirmation: I claim WISDOM now. Today, I refuse to be indecisive. I make the very best decisions based on what I know, and with WISDOM I am able to listen to my intuition to discern what to do in every situation, with ease and grace. ...

As you continue focusing on the light radiating from within you, it now delicately transforms into a shining silver color. ... This is your Power of WILL, shining at its highest, most elevated level. Divine WILL serves as your director, and brings you the Power to choose wisely. With WILL, you take your Understanding and Wisdom, and put them into action to be the best you can be. You make decisions to move forward in ways that are congruent with your values and spiritual Truths. ...

Take in this affirmation: I claim WILL now. Today, I make wise choices that are in alignment with my values and beliefs. I use WILL at the highest, most elevated level to direct my life. ...

As you continue focusing on the light radiating from within you, it now becomes a warm shade of olive green. ... This is your Power of ORDER, shining at its highest, most elevated level. Divine ORDER brings you the Power to organize and arrange everything in your life. With ORDER, you are able to prioritize, and keep everything in alignment ... including material things, actions, thoughts, and beliefs. ...

Take in this affirmation: I claim ORDER now. Today, I refuse to allow disorder, distractions, or multiple priorities to create frustration for me. I use ORDER to accomplish what needs to be done, when it needs to be done, in the easiest possible way. ...

As you continue focusing on the light radiating from within you, it now transforms into a deep, glowing russet brown. ... This is your Power of RELEASE, shining at its highest, most elevated level. Divine RELEASE brings you the Power to let go of anything that no longer serves you, joyfully opening up space for your personal enrichment and growth. RELEASE brings a sense of freedom as you eliminate everything you no longer use or need. ...

Life-Changing Spiritual Practices, Volume 1

Take in this affirmation: I claim RELEASE now. Today, I no longer allow obsolete things, ideas, or relationships to be present in my life. I use RELEASE to let go of anything that no longer serves me, creating space to breathe and grow. ...

As you continue focusing on the light radiating from within you, it now transforms into a brilliant vivid orange color. ... This is your Power of ZEAL, shining at its highest, most elevated level. Divine ZEAL brings you the Power of enthusiasm and excitement. With ZEAL, you bring passion and inspiration to everyone you meet and everything you do. Charles Fillmore, at age 94 said, "I fairly sizzle with zeal and enthusiasm and I spring forth with a mighty faith to do the things that need to be done by me." You have this Power of Zeal flowing now within you. ...

Take in this affirmation: I claim ZEAL now. Today, I sizzle with ZEAL and enthusiasm. I share my passion and inspire others to be a part of what I am doing. I have plenty of energy to make my dreams a reality. ...

As you continue focusing on the light radiating from within you, it now transforms into a gorgeous, rich shade of red. ... This is your Power of LIFE, shining at its highest, most elevated level. Divine LIFE brings you vitality and sustaining energy. With LIFE, you claim wholeness and health throughout your physical being, and you bring life to every project you undertake. ...

Take in this affirmation: I claim LIFE now. Today, my mind and body manifest Divine perfection. I bring LIFE to everything I do, as I express wholeness and vitality. I show up as my highest and best self! ...

Breathe deeply into the rainbow of color representing the 12 Divine Powers which are fully present within you right now. ... You have activated each of the Twelve Powers, and you are now operating from your highest, most elevated levels of those Powers. In this sacred moment, in this beautiful garden called your Consciousness, infused with the energy of the Twelve Powers, just be still and know ... you are holy ... you are worthy ... you are Divine ... you are God expressing at the point of you and you have within you everything you need to master the art of living, as you walk the spiritual path on practical feet.

And so it is!

(Recommended resource to support this practice: *Power Up Your Life: Accessing Your Twelve Powers to Achieve Health, Happiness, Abundance, and Inner Peace*, by Cher Holton, Bil Holton, and Paul Hasselbeck)

© 2014 Bil and Cher Holton, YourSpiritualPractice.com

Be Kind to Animals

Be kind to animals. All animals deserve to be treated humanely—family pets and wildlife. Animals are spiritual beings. They are healers, protectors, and playmates. You can trust that your pet's soul has been drawn to you in order to benefit from your level of consciousness and support you on your spiritual journey. If you own a pet and/or enjoy being around animals, you have, no doubt, felt that there is wonderful natural and harmonious balance that exists between you and them.

Since animals connect with happiness and unhappiness, positivity and negativity, our pets help us become higher quality people. When we are receptive and aware of the conscious connection our pets have with us, we will be more willing to serve and care for them, which helps to quicken not only their soul evolution, but our own.

Animal cruelty and abuse is not only tragic for animals, but also an indicator that other forms of abuse and cruelty (such as domestic violence, over-all crime, and world unrest) are representative of our need to elevate our consciousness as a human race. Reporting animal abuse and cruelty signify our level of spiritual advancement and unwillingness to tolerate the shadow side of human nature.

Until one has loved an animal, a part of one's soul remains unawakened.
(Anatole France)

Here's How This Spiritual Practice Works:

Make it a conscious practice to be kind to animals. Mindfully create an inviting space in your yard and garden for butterflies, squirrels, hummingbirds, and other creatures. While animals like deer, bats, skunks, squirrels, and raccoons can be a nuisance, look for ways to coexist with animals or to protect your property humanely.

If you have house pets, take care of them as family members. Never leave your pet alone in a car. Spay or neuter your dog or cat. Adopt pets from an animal shelter. Never kick, hit, or spank a pet. Spend quality time with your pet. Use a non-choking collar on your dog or cat. Provide nutritious food and constant fresh water for your pets. Keep chocolate away from pets—it can poison them. Take pets for annual health exams and recommended vaccinations.

© 2000, 2014 Bil and Cher Holton, YourSpiritualPractice.com

Backpacking

Few settings are more inspiring for an outdoor spiritual practice than the wilderness backcountry. Backpack trekking brings out both your inner warrior and your shamanic instincts. Going out into nature is really going into your soul. It is soulcraft in natural settings. Backpacking in wilderness environments inspires feelings of awe and wonder.

Your intimate contact with this natural environment leads to thoughts about the spiritual meanings of things and the eternal processes that underwrite what you see and experience. Backpacking features an aloneness that can cure all loneliness.

Some of the insights you'll gain by backpacking are: learning the importance of traveling light, carrying water to stay hydrated, feeling a deep desire to remain in idyllic settings, respecting the interconnectedness of things, and sensing you have touched the Divine. Whether you call It God, the Eternal Presence, Spirit, the Universe, Divine Mind, the Source of All, or simply Nature, you know you want to experience more of It.

In *Nature and Spirituality*, Margaret Emerson captures the feeling of being outdoors: "Perhaps you quietly sit gazing out at a bank of low clouds wrapping themselves intimately around a mountain peak and something shifts in your soul—as if you have been lifted out of yourself to the mysterious nether reaches of the cold granite escarpment beyond that which you can see. It's as if you are at the cusp of learning the answer to a great mystery, a revelation that you can have without feeling you are losing yourself in the wilderness."

Here's How This Spiritual Practice Works:

Plan a backpacking trip, with the conscious intention of making it a spiritual experience. If backpacking is new for you, make your initial adventure close by and short. Remember, the focus is not on ruggedness, but on spiritual enrichment.

As you walk, focus on your surroundings. Be attentive to the sounds, smells, and textures you are experiencing. Allow your soul to be blessed by the richness of this adventure. Keep a journal to capture your feelings and insights as you travel.

If you should adopt this spiritual practice, be diligent and careful about being properly equipped, appropriately dressed, and focused on safety for your treks. Your preparation for your backpacking trips is an apt metaphor for preparing for the kind of life you want to live.

© 2010 Bil and Cher Holton, YourSpiritualPractice.com

Draft a Truth Seeker Bill of Rights

Draft a Truth Seeker Bill of Rights suitable for framing. For the sake of your spiritual growth and the strength of your Christ connection, we strongly encourage you to refrain from making this declaration a perfunctory exercise. Create a substantive document that expresses how you feel about protecting your right as a spiritual being who is matriculating through a human experience.

Here's How This Spiritual Practice Works:

Gather together a notepad, favorite pens that help you feel creative, and a cup of tea or coffee (that last item is not required, but it does enhance the experience!). Outline key areas that you feel are critical for your spiritual unfoldment. For example:

- What are the necessary conditions for your spiritual progress?
- What spiritual practices do you value above all others?
- Define your theology/belief system.
- Clearly articulate what you consider important about spiritual growth.
- On what spiritual matters will you not compromise?

Once you have created your list, edit it. Fine tune it. Polish it. Then, transform it into a personal Truth Seeker Bill of Rights document, on nice paper, using your favorite fonts or calligraphy. Frame it. Read it every day. Honor it!

As your consciousness expands, modify your Bill of Rights to reflect your current spirituality. It will be the developmental scaffolding you need to make your spiritual journey a successful one. It'll serve as your barometer as you monitor your spiritual growth.

© 2000 Bil and Cher Holton, YourSpiritualPractice.com

Book Study

We've seen this spiritual growth experience literally transform people's lives. People get excited when they read higher consciousness learning material. The excitement usually translates into action, which becomes contagious and rewarding. The insights you'll gain will help increase your awareness of the indivisible nature between your human self, other people's human selves, and the Divine Nature (your SuperSelf™, your Christ Self, the Extraordinary You) which unites all of us.

Here's How This Spiritual Practice Works:

When it comes to your spiritual growth, it's a good practice to become immersed in a good book that has a spiritual, metaphysical, theosophical, philosophical, quantum physics, neuroscience, cellular biology, and/or natural science theme. Select one as a personal book-of-the-month, bi-month, or quarter. At self-appointed times, find a quiet place where you won't be interrupted, grab one of your favorite drinks, sit for a while, and read.

Record major insights in your journal so you can revisit them whenever you need a spiritual boost. Identify what you read in the book that made an impact, and specifically ask yourself how you can use what you've read in your own life.

This spiritual practice can be done on your own, or with a very select group of people who share your level of interest in and understanding of spiritual enrichment.

© 1990 Bil and Cher Holton, YourSpiritualPractice.com

Life-Changing Spiritual Practices, Volume 1

Breathing Space

Concentrating on your breathing allows the rest of your body to relax itself. 'Breathing Space' breathing is a great way to relax in the moment and get the body into body, mind, and soul harmony. This spiritual practice is an excellent 'present moment' technique to keep you calm and centered.

It takes only about 30 seconds; however, you can (and probably will) choose to extend it longer.

Here's How This Spiritual Practice Works:

- Find a comfortable position: Lie on your back if that is comfortable, or sit in an upright position.
- Slowly relax your body.
- Inhale slowly (through your nose if possible). Inhale to a slow count of 5. Fill the lower part of your chest first, then the middle and top part of your chest and lungs. Be sure to do this slowly, over 8 to 10 seconds.
- Hold your breath for a second or two. Then quietly and easily relax and let the air out through your mouth, to a slow count of 5.
- Wait a few seconds and repeat this cycle.
- If you find yourself getting dizzy, then you are overdoing it. Slow down. Imagine yourself in a peaceful, unhurried state of mind.

You can continue this breathing technique for as long as you think it's necessary to ensure your calmness and composure.

© 2002 Bil and Cher Holton, YourSpiritualPractice.com

Burning Bowl

This Burning Bowl experience is about recognizing the tremendous power of ritual to transform your life. It's an act of releasing what you've outgrown or want to outgrow, to make room for your greater good *in a flash*.

We define a 'flash' as the amount of time it takes to symbolically erase fear, doubt, worry, and disappointment. When you place the small slip of paper or flash paper on which you have written what you want to release in a bowl and then light it, you symbolically extinguish the energy of negativity. It is gone ... in a flash!

Let us add a little depth to this activity with some further commentary for your meditation and reflection.

This 'flash,' this combustible moment, is possible when you have faith in the following statement: Matthew 11:29 (NRSV) says: *"Take my yoke upon you ... and you will find rest."* In the Metaphysical Gospel of Matthew, Matthew 11:29 says: "The more we discipline ourselves to follow Truth principles (take up the yoke), the less resistance we will have (we will find rest) in aligning our human self with our Higher Self." Rest, metaphysically, means 'freedom from error and the consequences of error.'

So, you can get rid of error thinking, you can find rest, in a flash, in a combustible moment, when you choose truth over error.

Have faith in this symbolic process. The fire of Truth incinerates error. Any time you burn error, symbolically or otherwise, you rewire your brain circuits. That alchemical process is symbolically represented in this Burning Bowl experience.

If you have faith enough in the power of ritual as an extension of your intention, you will be able to erase error from your consciousness—and transform your life—in a flash—because you will have rewired your neural circuits in a positive way.

This personal odyssey gives you an opportunity to take stock, and reflect on the things from your past that are no longer working for you, that are holding you back from experiencing your best and greatest good. Simply let them go, let them go, let them go!

What you choose to release can take many forms. For example:

- *Physical things:* Perhaps you desire more control and order in your life. So, release any "stuff" that is no longer serving you. Release and let go of the disorder in your files, or closets, or garage, or attic, or basement, or storage shed. Let it go!
- *Emotional things:* Are you holding onto any grudges? Do you find yourself still blaming someone in your past for your current state of affairs? Is anger or hurt festering deep within your heart center? Let it go!

- *Attitudes or beliefs:* Listen to the things you say to yourself. If you are hearing phrases like: I don't deserve…; I can't…; I never…; I wish I could…; I'm only; I'm too…" Let it go! Know that you are worthy—you are Divine! If you are hanging onto old beliefs that sabotage your spiritual progress, let them go!

Here's How This Spiritual Practice Works:

Pick up a small piece of notepad paper, flash paper, or a Post-It Note. Play soft music, as you consider what you want to release forever, in anticipation of the dramatic spiritual growth you will experience. Write the things you want to release—the things you are truly ready to let go of—on your paper. Then, when you are ready, place your paper in a glass bowl. Feel free to state either aloud or silently the affirmation: "I now release these things forever, and claim my greater good."

As you stand near the bowl, use a match or lighter to light your paper, releasing the energy to the Universe. (Stand at arm's length from the bowl.) Watch as what you have just released incinerates. Symbolically, you have eliminated it from your life. Bless your experience. Invite Spirit to whisper gently what is yours to do in terms of the spiritual, personal, and/or professional growth you want.

Take a deep God-breath as you center yourself and relax in the security and safety of this sacred moment. In this moment of quiet, go deep within your center of being, and ask your Higher Self to reveal what it is you most need to release, what you need to let go to make room for your greater good and your spiritual growth. In the silence, listen … and you will know.

KNOW:
As close as the wave is to the ocean;
As close as the flame is to the candle;
As close as your own breathing ~ That is how close the Eternal Universal Presence is—because YOU ARE the human expression of the Eternal Presence at the point of you.

So, let your light shine as you rekindle your inner Spirit and walk the spiritual path on practical, holy feet as you connect with the Extraordinary You, your Higher Self.

© 2001, 2007, 2010 Bil and Cher Holton, YourSpiritualPractice.com

Be Your Personal Change Master

Flexibility, a healthy acceptance for ambiguity, an uncanny ability to manage multiple priorities, a willingness to manage chaos, patience and foresight, and a penchant for newness are not only key prerequisites for mastering the art of living, but for being able to mature in your spirituality.

The pace of accelerated change is phenomenal. The amount of personal and professional elasticity and recuperative powers necessary to keep up with strobe-like change demand every ounce of your courage and faith.

Millions of people (or is that billions) have been derailed by changes in their environment because they failed to see or accept the inevitability of change. Prying some people loose from prehistoric beliefs, frozen, unyielding, cemented attitudes, outdated assumptions, and embedded theology takes considerable spiritually-inclined 'torque.'

Some outdated beliefs will have to be chemicalized out! (Chemicalization is the inner process that occurs when we have conflicting beliefs fighting within our consciousness. This often manifests as illness or emotional upsets.) One thing is for certain—anyone who fails to, refuses to, or intentionally recoils from change will dampen their spiritual progress and postpone their ability to connect with their True Self, their Higher Self. (Do we have your attention? We hope so!)

This spiritual practice calls for you to become your own personal change master. To untie Gordian Knots. To loosen up. To welcome change as a friend. To climb out of your self-imposed ruts (quickly we might add).

Life-Changing Spiritual Practices, Volume 1

Here's How This Spiritual Practice Works:

Begin by designing an incremental change program of your own. When? Now, of course! Immediately. Where? Where you are now—personally, professionally, spiritually. What does the program consist of? Positive changes. Small-step self exploration and improvement. Minuscule course corrections. Major turns. Inner child calisthenics. Self-renewal. Repotting yourself.

Some of our favorite calisthenics for enriching your spiritual practice are:
- Perform some routine act (i.e., brush your teeth, comb your hair, button your shirt or blouse, tie your shoes, etc.) with your non-dominant hand;
- enroll in a drama class;
- drive home a different way;
- adopt a new hobby that seems totally uncharacteristic of you;
- walk around the house or apartment barefooted;
- snuggle up to a potter's wheel and mold clay;
- enjoy an afternoon snooze in a hammock, lounge chair or recliner;
- if you like fried eggs, scramble them, hard boil 'em, or prepare them sunny side up;
- if you eat meat, go vegetarian for a day (or vice versa);
- within a reasonable time span eliminate an old, entrenched habit;
- refrain from wearing your watch for a couple of days.

Here are a few more ideas, to stimulate your creativity:
- fast for half a day, a day, or two days (after you've consulted your doctor);
- write your name (in cursive) with your non-dominant hand;
- draw a picture using your toes or your teeth, or both;
- walk barefooted in a stream or creek;
- stand in the longest line at the supermarket;
- re-channel your gamesmanship energies and play to lose (at least some of the time to a lesser-skilled opponent);
- wrap yourself up in a stimulating metaphysical book;
- give one (or more) of your material possessions away to someone who will appreciate your generosity;
- avoid watching the news for a day;
- do something you haven't ever done before (like complimenting your mother-in-law, or remembering your wedding anniversary, or admitting a mistake);
- get to work an hour earlier than usual;
- back into a parking space instead of pulling in front first;
- turn back the brightness knob and listen to the TV instead of watching it;
- draw two pictures simultaneously using both hands;
- eat dinner (breakfast, lunch) using your non-dominant hand.

Life-Changing Spiritual Practices, Volume 1

Oh—We've got to mention these, too:
- get rolphed;
- eat tofu (without gagging);
- drink a large glass of grapefruit juice;
- sail;
- splunk;
- parachute or sky dive;
- change your hair style (hair color);
- if you like to read murder mysteries, read biographies or historical novels (or vice versa);
- adopt a new craft or hobby;
- refrain from watching TV for a day (two days, a week, five minutes);
- give your cell phone a vacation for a day;
- visit a relative or friend who has a youngster and play a game of fish (Crazy Eights, Apples to Apples);
- write a poem or short story;
- play a round of golf (softball, putt putt);
- write out your definition of God (angels, the Holy Spirit, prayer);
- sing in the shower;
- participate in a sweat lodge;
- attend a drawing (oil painting, water color) class;
- download a couple of phone apps that 'speak to you;
- visit someone you know who is sick (in the hospital, under Hospice care);
- whistle one of your favorite tunes;
- participate in a karaoke sing-in;
- plant a plant in the yard (vase, planter);
- spend five minutes alone or with someone you trust and just laugh (no conversation, simply laugh out loud)…

Add your own ideas to this list. Each is a mini-rehearsal for expanding your horizons, for pushing your limits, for getting used to doing something different. Each re-writes the brain and strengthens the neural connections for adaptability and change, newness and flexibility, higher thought and spiritual acumen.

© 2001, 2004, 2009, 2014 Bil and Cher Holton, YourSpiritualPractice.com

Refrain From Cell Phone Saluting

Cell phone saluting, in social media language, represents our attempt to increase the chances of receiving a text and/or add smart phone bars when there is little to no reception by raising our phone up in the air thinking that we will miraculously gain more bars.

From a spiritual perspective, we use the phrase "Cell Phone Saluting" to symbolize our intent to summon the help of an anthropomorphic God in the sky. Refraining from 'cell phone saluting' means coming to the realization that there is no anthropomorphic deity in the sky with a white beard and dressed in a white robe, micro-managing the universe and watching every move you make!

A 'God out there' is a religious concept that must be outgrown. When you truly understand that, you won't be tempted to ask, beg, or petition a Goodie God in the sky (hold your phone up in the air thinking that you'll miraculously gain more bars) to answer your prayers. Why? Because you'll know that you are God expressing in human form as you!

That means you are one with the Eternal Presence (God). You'll realize there's no need to look 'out there' for what you want because you have the power within you to manifest your good.

Here's How This Spiritual Practice Works:

Become aware of how you pray, and the content of the things you say. Be on the lookout for:
- language that begs, bargains, or pleads for help;
- use of gender-specific terms that imply the Universal Substance is human (i.e., He/She/Mother-Father God);
- Attributing causation to some being separate and apart from yourself (i.e., the Devil made me do it; God gave me this idea).

As soon as you catch yourself falling into the "Spiritual Cell Phone Saluting" trap, disconnect that call! Take a few deep breaths, center yourself, and affirm the Truth of who you are, claiming the essence of whatever it is you are desiring, knowing it is yours by right of Consciousness.

© 2014 Bil and Cher Holton, YourSpiritualPractice.com

Get Clear About Crossing Over

This spiritual practice helps you answer what we believe to be one of the most significant questions you will ask yourself as you evolve into your spirituality. Look in the mirror and ask the person you see: *"Have you crossed over yet?"* It is a question that defines where you are on your spiritual journey. The 'crossing over' we're referring to is not in the context of near death experiences, out-of-the-body experiences, or psychic readings and séances, although that's generally what the question above refers to when it comes to paranormal human experiences.

The 'crossing over' this practice refers to is this: ***"Have you crossed over yet ... from a religious mindset into a spiritual mindset?"*** Have you moved beyond the dogma, exclusivity, close-mindedness, and anthropomorphic godism associated with the embedded theology of your religious up-bringing into the open-mindedness, inclusivity, eclectic nature, and friend of science perspective of spirituality?

Getting clear about crossing over opens up new vistas for your spiritual growth and continuing enlightenment. There's no need to apply dogmatic brakes because there's nothing to brake for when it comes to adding to your spiritual resume.

Here's How This Spiritual Practice Works:

Seat yourself in front of a mirror and ask yourself: "Have you crossed over yet?" Then take some dedicated time to reflect on what that question means to you, and how you would answer it, in the context of your current spiritual growth.

Then reflect on this next set of questions:
- Do you see yourself as more spiritual than religious?
- Have you outgrown Bible basics, Torah basics, and Koran basics because you believe there are deeper meanings to scriptural passages than their literal interpretations?
- Are you open to teachings that focus on original blessings instead of original sin?
- Do you believe you are a spiritual being having a human experience?
- Do you believe you don't have to die to go to heaven—or hell—because they are both current states of consciousness that you can experience in this now moment?

If you answered 'yes' to this second set of questions, you have 'crossed over' from religion into spirituality. You have moved from limitation to expansiveness, from dogmatic blinders to questioning stale religious beliefs, from mindless indoctrination to intuitive knowing and transcendental experiencing.

That's what this spiritual practice is all about—introspectively measuring where you are and how much you've outgrown your religious identity. As Unity ministers who have moved to being more spiritual than religious, we can tell you it feels really good to be religiously spiritual! It's a freeing perspective. And once you've crossed over (once your mind has been stretched by a new and compelling spiritual mindset), you no longer want to go back to a religious straightjacket.

© 2015 Bil and Cher Holton, YourSpiritualPractice.com

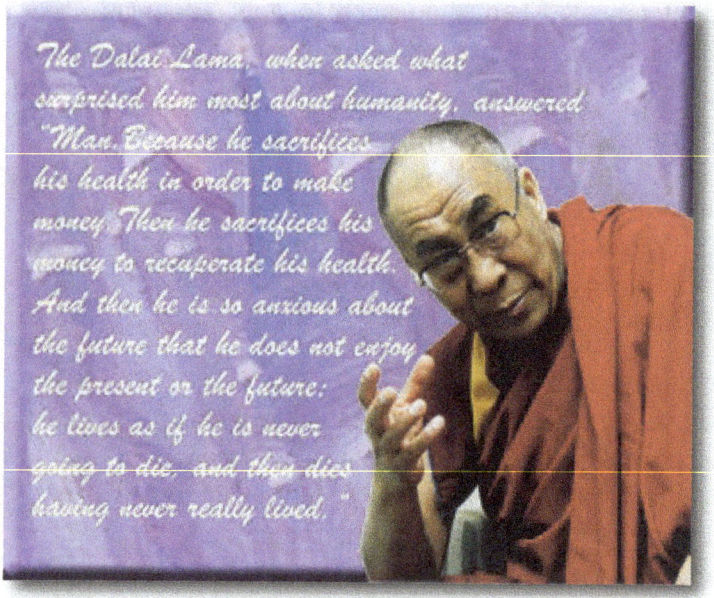

Celebrate Small Wins

Celebrating small wins is a good practice for two reasons. It keeps you focused on the positive, life-affirming choices you make and it reminds you of the continuous improvements you are making to connect with your True Self, your Authentic Self.

How long should you make celebrating small wins a practice? It's up to you, of course; but our immediate response is: how long and how often do you want to make direct contact with your Higher Self, the Extraordinary You?

Here's How This Spiritual Practice Works:

Find at least one tiny event to celebrate each week. It can be some spiritual practice you have started or restarted ... some modification in lifestyle that amplifies your spiritual resume.

Here are some soul-deepening examples just off the top of our heads and from the bottom of our hearts:

- a healthy change in your diet;
- reading the spiritual book or watching the spiritual DVD that's been collecting dust on your bookshelf at home since you purchased it;
- deciding to forgive someone;
- catching yourself being too negative, and replacing those thoughts with positive affirmations.

If it's an old habit that you've put to rest, celebrate its dismissal by adopting a new, spiritually-oriented one in its place. Give yourself a pat on the back for writing a new affirmation or finding time in your busy schedule to meditate, pray, or read a spiritual quote or two. Learn a new mantra or add breathing exercises to stimulate the neurons in your brain. Whatever it is, celebrate with intention and gusto!

© 2001, 2004, 2009, 2014 Bil and Cher Holton, YourSpiritualPractice.com

Life-Changing Spiritual Practices, Volume 1

Chanting / Reciting Mantras

Chanting meaningful spiritual words or phrases is one of the easiest spiritual practices to follow. It has the ability to heal at a cellular level and purify not just your physical body, but also your mental and emotional attributes. You can chant anywhere. It is not restrained by time, place, loudness, or softness. There are many forms of chanting: kirtan chanting (call and response chanting), Buddhist chanting, vedic chanting, Sikh chanting, Bhakti chanting, etc.

Chanting helps quiet mind chatter, which we call 'chatter bombs.' The intellect is a great evolutionary tool, the product of tens of thousands of years of skin school experience. Unfortunately, it likes to be engaged all of the time. Chanting bypasses the intellect and short-circuits its incessant chatter.

While chanting can seem boring, it has a profound effect on your consciousness. The repetitive sounds of chanting entrain your body's energy centers to the rhythm of the chant. The repetitious pulses shift your state of being into greater alignment with your divine nature. Your heart rate lowers and your blood pressure also lowers. Your breath capacity increases.

Not only is chanting a form of prayer and meditation, it is also an extremely useful adjunct to other spiritual practices. Because of its powerful ability to calm the mind, chanting can serve as a relaxation and centering tool as well, which makes it an excellent spiritual practice.

Here's How This Spiritual Practice Works:

Choose a spiritual word or short phrase that is particularly meaningful to you (i.e., peace, God, love, inner peace, Om, peace be still, etc.).

Find a comfortable position, and begin repeating this word or phrase over and over, until you achieve a rhythm. Allow the vibrations of the chant to flow through your being, and allow yourself to become totally absorbed in the experience.

Another option for this practice is to find musical chants that are recorded, and sing with them. Karen Drucker is one artist we enjoy who has created some wonderful chants.

You come fully equipped with the most magnificent instrument for opening the heart and sending your prayers soaring to the heavens: your own voice! Chanting as a spiritual practice is free, safe, and easy. You can chant in the car while commuting to work, chant to your heart's content in the shower, chant while sitting on your deck or balcony, chant while preparing your meals, chant while cleaning your house or apartment, and chant in your meditation room.

© 2006 Bil and Cher Holton, YourSpiritualPractice.com

Communing With Nature

Our daily environments are filled with ringing phones, alarms of one type or another, the incessant chatter on TV's and radios, sirens, horns, the sound of traffic—all of which hijack our attention and keep us preoccupied with the pulse of the city.

By contrast, natural environments are characterized by gentleness of the landscape, the serenity which envelops us as we wander down a tree-hewn path or see the valley below from a mountaintop, the awesome connectedness we feel wading barefoot through a cascading brook, and the reverence that penetrates our very being as we stand a few feet from a doe and her young.

Taking a break from technological environments and stepping into the cocoon of nature is revitalizing and refreshing. It is to be nurtured by Gaia's embrace. Echopsychologists remind us that our deepest roots are in nature, and the factories and silicone environments we have invented are but subsystems of the biosphere.

Helen Keller teases us with her reveling about nature when she says, "What a joy it is to feel the soft, springy earth under my feet once more, to follow grassy roads that lead to ferny brooks where I can bathe my fingers in a cataract of rippling notes, or to clamber over a stone wall into green fields that tumble and roll and climb in riotous gladness!"

And Thich Nhat Hanh assures us that we "inter-breathe with the rain forests and drink from the oceans. They are part of our own body."

The shift from invigorating outdoor activities by choosing sedentary, indoor technology-driven activities has already shown far-reaching consequences for our physical and mental health. Videophilia (electronic addiction) has been shown to cause obesity, contribute to a lack of socialization, elevate blood pressure and hypertension, and contribute to an overall sense of lethargy and listlessness.

On the biochemical level, spending time with nature stimulates our feel-good neurotransmitters like dopamine, serotonin, and endorphins. It turns off the sympathetic nervous system, improves our moods and brain function, decreases pain, heightens feelings of well-being and connectedness, and reduces stress. Communing with nature on a regular basis is an excellent spiritual practice for nourishing and renewing ourselves and optimizing our mental, physical and spiritual health.

In *The Experience of Nature: A Psychological Perspective*, researchers Rachel and Steven Kaplan describe what they call "the restorative experience." It seems that the experience of being in nature is transformative in and of itself. It contributes to a person's emotional state being uplifted and mental balance being restored. Communing in nature is truly empowering in a very deep, meaningful way.

The Kaplans concluded that: "The experience of nature, whether passively observed or actively participated in, is an important component of psychological well-being."

It is extremely interesting to note that research from Herriot-Watt University, which used advanced technology to measure brain waves through mobile EEGs, shows what spiritual teachers and philosophers have intuitively known for generations—that a walk in the park may be the most beneficial thing we can do for our mental, physical, emotional health and spiritual well-being.

Here's How This Spiritual Practice Works:

This spiritual practice invites you to get in touch with nature. It can be something as simple as watching a sunset or sunrise, observing cloud formations, or gazing at the moon and stars. Let the warm summer breeze caress your hair and skin, allow a babbling brook to nurture your senses, hypnotize yourself with the soft patter of rain falling on leaves nearby, or notice the mystical silence of snowflakes as they fall.

Hug a tree. Lie on the grass. Sit on a rock. Walk barefooted in a stream. Listen to the chorus of birds. Talk to squirrels, rabbits, deer, and insects. Coo at a dove. Mimic the cry of a crow. Feel the texture of leaves and ferns. Listen to the hoot of an owl. Feel your connectedness to the natural world.

Relish the peace and tranquility you feel in the midst of a glen or meadow. Notice the alignment you sense with something deep within you that speaks to you at a soul level, telling you that there is more to your relationship with nature than meets the eye.

Build nature walks and outings into your spiritual practice. Make them regular spiritual exercises.

© 1983, 2006 Bil and Cher Holton, YourSpiritualPractice.com

Consult Your Crystal Ball

While we advocate that we each have a crystal ball within, where we can retrieve the best guidance and advice for any issue we are facing, this spiritual practice encourages you to strengthen your own inner guidance system by consulting the crystal balls of other spiritual giants and people whom you consider to be spiritually mature and authentic.

Here's How This Spiritual Practice Works:

Purposefully and systematically meet with people whom you consider to be spiritually mature and authentic. Ask them about their spiritual journey and spiritual growth practices. Inquire how they organize their day around spiritual themes and which spiritual practices have been the most helpful. Ask how they juggle daily responsibilities and spiritual priorities. Ask how their dedication to their spirituality has helped them connect with their SuperSelf™ their Extraordinary Nature.

YouTube, watch DVD's, documentaries, and TV specials, and read about highly spiritual people in various faith traditions. Record the qualities and similarities that make these people such spiritual giants.

Thoroughly examine your own truth walk. Make the changes you feel you need to make. Adopt spiritual practices that amplify your own truth walk. Strengthen your spiritual resume.

Visualize how your new and improved spiritual practice will look. Check your crystal ball. Realize that you, too, can become a spiritual giant.

© 1990, 2014 Bil and Cher Holton, YourSpiritualPractice.com

Life-Changing Spiritual Practices, Volume 1

Your Daily Red and Bread

This spiritual practice is based on the Gospel of Mark 14:12-26. However, you don't have to consult the traditional Biblical passage to use this practice as a personal ritual, because this practice is based on the metaphysical interpretation of that passage. We also have a group spiritual practice based on the same Biblical passage, but this individual experience is totally different. It is designed as your individual ceremony to honor your indivisible connection with your Divine Nature.

Your individual ceremony can take 8-10 minutes (reading the metaphysical interpretation below, preparing and partaking of the elements, and taking time for a brief meditation) or it can take longer, depending on the length of your meditation. You will be reading an annotated reading, so scriptural wording from the Gospel of Mark will appear in parentheses.

You will see that we use the Christ terminology since the metatranslation is taken from Mark's Gospel. However, we see the Christ designation as the same as Buddhahood, Krishnahood, your I AM Nature, etc.

Here's How This Spiritual Practice Works:

Gather together a small glass of red grape juice (or wine, if you are so inclined) and a small piece of bread. You may want to light a candle and/or play some soft music to create a meditative environment. Once you are ready, settle into a quiet, comfortable location, and spend some time breathing into this experience. When you feel that heart connection, you are ready to begin reading Mark 14:12-26. We invite you to use the metaphysical version of the text below, recognizing that it represents your spiritual path toward enlightenment:

> *When your spiritual growth evolves to the point that you are on the brink of attaining Christhood, your heightened consciousness will produce a telling energetic effect on perfecting your body, mind, and soul (unleavened bread). You may wonder how best to prepare yourself for such a transformation. Initially, you must take a balanced spiritual approach (two disciples) into your daily living (city) and discover that you can manage (carry a jar) your emotions (water). There is no need to doubt your ability to maintain your composure because your Higher Self knows when the "turning*

point" which heralds your Christship—enlightenment—will take place. It is important to remember that at the level of Spirit (large room upstairs, furnished and ready) you are already a Christed being. So, your chief task in life is to prepare yourself for your greater good by keeping yourself Christ-centered each-consecutive-moment-of-now.

As you near the completion of your current cusp of consciousness, you will notice how evolved your higher spiritual qualities (disciples) have become. And while you attempt to understand (eat) your newly-acquired state of consciousness, you may sense an element of betrayal because there is a part of you that is still attached to materiality, particularly since you have allowed most of your previous thinking to be ruled by a materialistic ego. The Christ of you is aware that you are a spiritual being in human form (dipping bread) and a human being spiritually formed (the bowl called human experience). Through your Christed Self you will be able to discern the difference between Truth and error. You are entirely responsible—and accountable—for your thoughts, words, choices and actions. If you choose error (betrayal) over Truth, your spiritual void will be greater because your fall from grace will be greater.

When you internalize (eat) the full implications of the Omnipresence of Divine Substance (bread), you will transcend any and all beliefs in limitation. And when you have risen completely above the attachments of an unenlightened ego (drink from cup), you will experience an incredible 'transfusion of consciousness' (blood of the covenant poured out) whereby you receive a purer strain of Divine Consciousness. When you achieve that level of sanctification, your Christhood is assured. As an illumined being in the making (the singing of the hymn) your life will become a symphony of wisdom, love, and joy (a Mount of Olives experience).

After reading this passage, you may dip the bread in the juice/wine you have prepared and eat it slowly and meditatively, silently honor your God connection. You may also use this time for a brief meditation to express your oneness with your Christ Essence.

We repeat this practice once a month, except during the Lenten season, when we honor our 'transfusion in consciousness' every day.

© 2012 Bil and Cher Holton, YourSpiritualPractice.com

Life-Changing Spiritual Practices, Volume 1

Dancing

In her delightful book, *Dance—The Sacred Art: The Joy of Movement*, Cynthia Winton-Henry assures you that "If you're thinking, 'But I'm not a dancer' or 'I feel awkward,' I hope to reassure you that you don't need a special talent to move. You don't need to be graceful or especially coordinated. You don't need a body that's 'in shape.' Dance connects you to the movement of life. Dance is not just a novel way to illustrate beliefs and theology, nor is it dumbed-down prayer. It is a completely different way of knowing the Holy. It hints at the divine dance to which we are all invited."

Many people, however, have a hard time believing dancing is spiritual. They seem burdened with feelings of awkwardness and self-consciousness when it comes to dancing. Dance, as a legitimate spiritual practice, lets your movement come from the inside out. It means your intent is not to look good, but to express your goodness via joyful movement.

Here's How This Spiritual Practice Works:

Choose your favorite music, and key it up. You'll want to do this spiritual practice in a room where you have lots of space to move around.

Take a few moments to breathe into your heart center, then let the music play. Dance to the music, allowing your body to flow with what you are hearing. There is no right way to do this! Simply let the music take over your body, and go with the flow.

If you feel clumsy, for instance, let that clumsiness be a part of your uninhibited movement. As you glide across the floor, try exaggerating your movements. Be playful. Sing with the melody. Smile. Laugh. Lose yourself in the dance so that your movements are without any forethought, hesitation, or embarrassment.

There are Praise Dances, Ritual Dances, Circle Dances, Meditative Dances, Cultural Sacred Dances, and Ecstatic Dances, to name a few, from every religious and spiritual tradition. What dancing as a spiritual practice is really about is for you to become one with the music, the movement, and letting all 'trying to do it right' thoughts which surface go, so you can enjoy dance as a soulful spiritual practice.

Our favorite group dancing spiritual practice is ballroom dancing. It is a partnership dance that brings us great joy and happiness. We invite you to find a dance style that is perfect for you, one that connects you with your divine nature. Partnership dancing is a wonderful spiritual discipline, but so is dancing by yourself.

© 1984 Bil and Cher Holton, YourSpiritualPractice.com

Life-Changing Spiritual Practices, Volume 1

Routine Daily Activities

Believe it or not, routine daily activities can be moments of spiritual connection. Life itself is a spiritual practice when you look at each moment as an opportunity to experience your oneness with your Higher Self. You can turn the simple things you do everyday into mini spiritual practices.

Here's How This Spiritual Practice Works:

Transform routine tasks into an opportunity for Mindful Focus. Whatever you perform, do it slowly, being aware of every move, every scent, every sensation. Allow yourself to become fully immersed in the activity.

For instance, routines like the following can be 'cameos' of spirituality in action if, while doing them, you become aware of their soulful nature and their relationship to your present moment being and doing: changing the sheets on your bed; pre-prayering the next day before you go to sleep; making sure all the house lights are turned off before going to bed; showering and/or bathing; brushing and flossing your teeth; taking creature comfort breaks; combing and/or brushing your hair; getting dressed or undressed; preparing and eating breakfast; rinsing and loading the dishes for the dishwasher and/or washing the dishes by hand; checking emails; buying groceries; putting groceries away when you get home; walking from the parking lot to your office or work station; taking your lunch hour at work; opening mail; paying bills; playing electronic games on your iPad or smart phone; chatting with family and friends on the phone; etc.

Immerse yourself in the nowness of whatever you're doing. Become fully engaged in these 'cameo' activities. Pay attention to their value in spite of their habitualness, in relation to your healthy and harmonious daily functioning. One of the reasons these spiritual practices are so important is that becoming enlightened includes being aware of present moment living and the value each-consecutive-moment-of-now has on your spiritual unfoldment.

© 1986, 2013 Bil and Cher Holton, YourSpiritualPractice.com

Defriending Dogma

*D*ogma is a set of religious principles, teachings, and beliefs presented by parochial authorities as being incontrovertibly true. They cannot be changed, discarded, or challenged by the faithful. All religions have dogmas and they are considered core principles that must be upheld by all believers of that particular religion. As a matter of fact, rejection of a given dogma may lead to expulsion from a religious group.

Whenever you hear the word 'doctrine,' it is referring to dogma. In his commencement address at Yale University, June 11 1962, John F. Kennedy summed up dogma pretty well: "Too often we hold fast to the clichés of our forebears. We subject all facts to a prefabricated set of interpretations. We enjoy the comfort of opinion without the discomfort of thought."

Steve Jobs had this to say about the importance of defriending dogma:

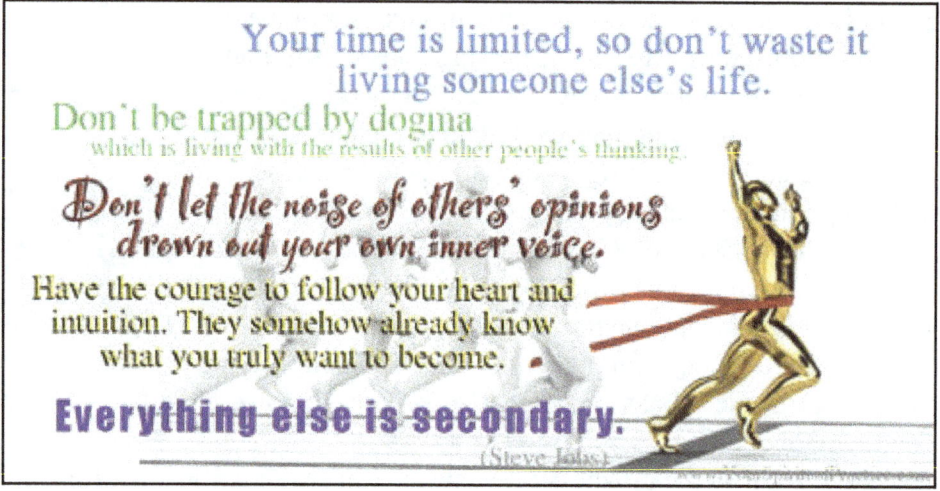

Sharon Salzberg, co-founder with Jack Kornfield of the Insight Meditation Society, has a similar view about the pitfalls of dogmatic thinking, "I think so many people tend to think of faith as blind adherence to a dogma or unquestioned surrender to an authority figure, and the result is losing self-respect and losing our own sense of what is true."

Here's How This Spiritual Practice Works:

Question what you believe—and what others tell you to believe! Follow the advice of Steve Jobs as a spiritual practice! Defriending dogma as a spiritual practice will be one of your chief lifelong spiritual growth strategies. Employ it well.

© 2014 Bil and Cher Holton, YourSpiritualPractice.com

Drawing / Painting

In Frederick Franck's book, *Zen Seeing, Zen Drawing*, he tells us the secret of why we must draw. He says, "You may tenderly trace the lines of your toes or a lady bug or a weed in the garden. You see", he says, "it isn't about the skill or talent that we believe an artist needs to come here with, it's about the ability to truly see—to slow down and see. And we each (as we know) have our own quirky way of seeing things. This accounts for the uniqueness of what we will create. This is the gift we bring to the world on many levels."

Drawing and other forms of artwork are ancient and universal languages used to express how we see the world and to find ways of healing. Drawing is a natural activity that most of us have shut away with memories of childhood.

The theologian and artist Jeremy Begbie writes that, "The urge to make and enjoy art seems to be universal: the impulse to scratch out images on stone walls, revel in the delight of notes strung together, shape and re-shape words into patterns, and so on. These activities go beyond entertainment and self-expression. They reveal, disclose, open up the world we live in, and in unique ways. They can be vehicles of discovery."

Drawing, like all of the arts, is rooted in a physical process, providing us with an increased awareness of our senses. It helps us bypass critical, left-brain thinking and respond from our sensual awareness. It also gives us creative ways to express our relationship with the world of appearances.

Creativity is 'the process of bringing something new into being,' something that did not exist before—an idea, a new arrangement, a drawing, a painting, a story. Our creations, which are new realities, work to enlarge our ways of seeing, feeling, and sensing the world and human consciousness with what is possible.

Here's How This Spiritual Practice Works:

One of the ways which we can take advantage of drawing as a spiritual practice is to use art-making as a form of spiritual expression. In art-making we engage the creative process consciously as a sacred experience which demonstrates our indivisibleness with our God essence.

There are many types of drawing: touch drawing (invented by Deborah Koff-Chapin), water coloring, pen and ink drawing, charcoal drawing, crayon and highlighter drawing, pencil drawing, and so on. Try a variety of mediums. See which ones resonate with you. Create something from the inside out! Then reflect on the message your drawing has for you.

© 1988, 1998, 2014 Bil and Cher Holton, YourSpiritualPractice.com

An In-Depth Reading: Fasting From Error

You will find this treatment of the concept of 'fasting' a bit different, perhaps, than what you've been used to. So, make sure you're sitting in a comfortable chair, and read through our version of "fasting."

One of the common practices among people in general (religious, spiritual, and even non-religious) is to "Fast" during Lent. But before we share our ideas about the practice of fasting in a spiritual context, we'd like to share some connotations of the word 'fast' that might interest you, which have nothing to do with curbing your appetite. Think about this:

People are fast when they can run rapidly;
But things are fast when they are tied down and fixed in place.
And colors are fast when they do not run at all.
A friend who is loyal is fast;
But someone who moves in suspect company is also called fast ~
And this is a little different from playing fast and loose.
Fast food is called fast when it's quick and easy to prepare,
And yet it's called fasting when we refrain from eating at all!
A watch is fast when it is running ahead of time,
And we are fast asleep when we are totally unaware of time!
When we hold fast to a rope, we want to hang on,
But when our foot is stuck fast in a hole, we want to get it free!
Photographic film is fast when it is sensitive to light,
But bacteria are fast when they are insensitive to antiseptics!
(We could go on, but we want to keep this spiritual practice fast paced).

Our perspective on fasting as Unity ministers is simple—**We advocate fasting from those toxic thoughts, beliefs, and attitudes that create an illusion of separation between you and your innate divinity!** What we want to focus on is some prep work! You know, like when you join a gym, and you're so anxious to get on the cool equipment—and the trainer says, "Not so fast! You need to warm up first!" (Cher always hated that warm up time, and yet she came to learn the value of it.) Just as you do some warm ups to prepare for singing or exercise, there is a special way we want to prepare to fast, to be in alignment with our Higher Self!

So—what does our "Warm Up" consist of?

First of all, warm up by making time to go to Headquarters—everyday! Entering into a time of fasting means you are going to be transforming your way of thinking and being, and creating huge shifts in your own consciousness. To do this, you really need to be in a state of oneness with your innate divinity, your Christ nature, the Extraordinary You. This comes only from that time spent in Headquarters, in the Silence.

The Christ as Jesus knew this. He spent 40 days alone in the wilderness as He prepared to begin His ministry, during which time, in the literal translation, He was tempted by Satan. This is a very powerful story (Matthew 4:1-11). The metaphysical essence of it is simply this (and we're sharing from Bil's *Gospel of Matthew: New Metaphysical Version*): The attainment of a higher spiritual consciousness is generally followed by thoughts from our sense consciousness which reject our oneness with Spirit and express themselves as earthly temptations. The best way to handle such spiritually corrosive thoughts is to retreat forward into prayer and meditation for the strength needed to address these enticements." In other words, prepare for your fasting!

The other really important preparation for fasting is to choose to live in JOY! If you talk to people during the Lenten season, they like to brag about how miserable they are during their period of fasting and how they can't wait until Lent is over, when they can jump back into their old habits.

Our perspective is a little different: we believe that, since we are fasting from anything that separates us from our oneness with Spirit, we can feast on joy! In fact, we base this on Matthew 6:16-18, when Jesus instructed: *"When you fast, don't look all gloomy, so everyone knows you're fasting."* (In other words, if it's just a façade, the fasting means nothing! And there's no lasting impact from it). *"But when you fast, put oil on your head and wash your face, so that it will not be obvious to others that you are fasting ... God, who sees what is done in secret, will reward you."* (In other words, when we allow ourselves to model the absolute joy of our oneness with the Eternal Presence, allowing our light to shine as a result of fasting from error thinking, we will be rewarded with the growing consciousness of divine flow in our lives).

One of those rewards, we believe, is a quickened understanding and awareness of higher truth principles. Several days ago, Cher woke up really early and decided to go into our Meditation Room, and do some journaling and meditation. Following the meditation, she picked up Myrtle Fillmore's *Healing Letters*, and did what she often does—she affirmed that she would open to a reading section that would be of guidance and help to her as she began her day. Then she just opened the book, looked down, and underlined on the page were these words: *"It is a common error among us that we do not exercise, rest, work, eat, and drink as we should. ... Healing will come through taking the right mental attitude, and getting right down into the body and telling it the Truth; then following up this treatment daily with sensible and scientific living habits."* Wow! What a perfect preparation for fasting! Not to deprive ourselves of certain foods, but to joyfully feed our very being with all that is healthy, good, and true! What could be better than that?

One of the secrets to connecting with the Extraordinary You is fasting from anything that is self-negating. It is being willing to move beyond false assumptions and beliefs—to be open to truth no matter how much it upsets conventional apple carts.

What Do We Need to Outgrow to Master the Art of Living?

If we want to master our human experience, we've got to move beyond the fiction imposed upon us by convention. When it comes to religious matters, we must absolutely positively outgrow the embedded theology we were taught.

As you move into Lent, Easter, or any other time of the year, there are a few myths we want to expose. They've been around a long time and people continue to be misled by them. For example,

- We must outgrow the myth that Jesus was God's Only Begotten Son who came to earth to save us. The truth is he was a carpenter's son from Nazareth who fulfilled his Christ potential. He is not so much the great exception as He is the great example. Like Jesus we can all become one with our Christ Self, our SuperSelf™, our True Self.
- We must outgrow the myth of original sin, and embrace the truth of original blessing. We are not unworthy sinners. We are God expressing at the point of us.
- We must outgrow the myth that we have to die to go to Heaven. The truth is Heaven is a state of consciousness. It is not a place up there. It is a state of being in here. (We're pointing to our heads and hearts). There is no white-haired man in the sky watching our every move, nor a red-tailed devil tempting us.
- On a lighter note we must outgrow the myth that if we don't put on a jacket in cold weather we'll catch a cold. The truth is the "common cold" is caused by the rhinovirus and it doesn't matter if you're wearing a coat or not.
- We must outgrow the myth that if we swallow gum it'll take seven years to pass through our digestive system! The truth is we will pass the gum in a day or two like we pass everything else down there.
- We must outgrow the myth that our happiness and security are determined by the economy. The truth is our greater good comes from the strength of our God connection.
- This next one may surprise you. We must outgrow the myth, once and for all, that Easter is all about suffering. The truth is it is about our complete mastery over error consciousness.

Jesus Christ is the Roger Bannister of Enlightenment. Roger Bannister was the first man to run a sub-four minute mile. Jesus became fully conscious of his Christhood and showed us how He did it! Because he fulfilled His divine potential, we can too!

If we truly understood Easter it would be a bigger holiday than Christmas. Christmas symbolizes the birth of the awareness of our Christ Nature. Easter represents the full and complete demonstration of our Christhood.

Unfortunately, as Easter is practiced by many fundamental faith traditions today, it falls short of that understanding.

Life-Changing Spiritual Practices, Volume 1

The traditional practice of Lent calls for us to "deprive ourselves of pleasure." The focus, as we said earlier, is on giving up things like chocolate, ice cream, soft drinks, doughnuts, potato chips, and so on. The phrase "deny yourself" is the catch phrase.

This 'ash and sackcloth perspective' is designed to deprive us of pleasures and asks us to impose some sort of voluntary suffering into our lives. And because it's a product of embedded theology, it uses Jesus' suffering and crucifixion to justify our own suffering and sacrifice.

Ash Wednesday & Fasting—From a Spiritual Perspective

Conventional Ash Wednesday services use the symbolism of putting ashes on our foreheads to remind us of our unworthiness, sinfulness, and need for redemption. The prophet Jeremiah called for Israel to "wallow in ashes" (Jer.6:26).

This rather juvenile view of Ash Wednesday focuses on sinfulness, sorrow, unnecessary sacrifices, unworthiness, and repentance. Our Ash Wednesday perspective is completely different. We place oil on people's foreheads to celebrate their divinity.

In his classic book, *Keep a True Lent*, Charles Fillmore, co-founder of Unity, makes an extraordinary statement, a myth-busting statement:

> *It is commonly believed that Lent has to do with the events of the forty days preceding the Resurrection of Christ. This is an erroneous idea. Lent is a church institution, and there is no authorization for it anywhere in the New Testament. The idea, however, has a sound spiritual basis. Moses, Elijah, and Jesus set precedents for it. Each observed a period of prayer and fasting as a preparation for their spiritual work.*

We are here to assure you that it is an erroneous belief to deprive yourself of simple pleasures during Lent or at any other time. We're going to go even further and say it is absurd to fast from comfort foods and simple pleasures as penance for your supposed unworthiness and sinful nature.

From a Christ-centric level of consciousness there is only one kind of fasting: fasting from error thoughts, words, and actions. The dieting we advocate is dieting from any doubts you may have about your ability to live an extraordinary life; fasting from any fears you may have about losing your job or finding a new one in a topsy turvy economy; abstaining from the belief that you aren't meant to have more or that you'll never be prosperous; fasting from religious myths and perspectives that denigrate you and cause you to doubt your worth—that is our message.

Fasting for forty days during Lent is a metaphor. Metaphysically speaking, forty days means wholeness, completion, fullness. It doesn't have anything to do with forty calendar days.

We encourage you to fast from the belief that you are too old, too young, too tired, too financially burdened, too unsure of your future, or too strapped with bad habits to master the art of living.

Fast from the belief that life has to be filled with suffering and struggle, and unemployment, and an empty wallet.

The Christ as Jesus did not say in John 10:10—"I came that you might have suffering, and difficulties, and health challenges, and failed relationships, and money problems, and pimples." He said—"I came that you might have LIFE and have it more abundantly."

The kind of life He was talking about is a life of peace, health, happiness, wholeness, joy, unlimited prosperity, and abundance.

So you see, from a higher consciousness perspective, Lent goes well beyond the fossilized myths about Easter. Lent is a spiritual retreat forward, a time of preparation, cleansing, and introspection. It's a time to fast from error, not dark chocolate. (If you've got a piece of chocolate lying around, eat it).

Any religious practice which denies simple pleasures and asks you to suffer and pay penance because you are a sinner misses the whole point of Easter.

Easter is a time to get serious about your divinity. It is a time to affirm that you have the power to master the art of living. It is a time to walk the spiritual path on practical, positive, progressive feet. It is the time to connect with your SuperSelf™, the Extraordinary You which is your Higher Self.

It's a time to eat a little dark chocolate.

© 2003, 2010 Bil and Cher Holton, YourSpiritualPractice.com

Footprints in the Sand (Our Version)*

You are probably familiar with the poem entitled *Footprints in the Sand*, written by Mary Stevenson in 1939. It shares a dream where the person sees footprints in the sand, recognizing that when there were two sets of footprints, God is walking beside him/her. But it seemed that during the roughest periods in this person's life, there was only one set of footprints. The dreamer questioned where God was, and God replied, "That is when I carried you."

We have adapted this popular poem to reflect a more spiritual perspective that aligns with our belief system. It acknowledges the Oneness we have with the Divine, and how we can choose to call on our Inner Power to harness the resources of the Field of Infinite Potential.

Here's How This Spiritual Practice Works:

Read and reflect on this version with an open mind and a spiritually-attuned heart. Think of your oneness and indivisibleness with the Eternal Presence:

One night I was walking contemplatively along the beach. I stood for a moment, closed my eyes, and saw many mental images of my life experiences flash across my mind. Then images of footprints in the sand appeared as if to footnote my mental visions.

Sometimes there were two sets of footprints, other times there was one set of footprints. This confused me because I noticed that during low periods in my life, when I was going through what I considered to be tough times, I could distinctly see two sets of footprints. Then I had one of those 'Aha' moments:

I said loud to myself, "When I forget who I really am, I slip back into the embedded theology I grew up on, and in the most trying periods of my life there seem to be two sets of footprints in the sand.

"When I neglect to pay attention to the truth principles I have studied, I fall into the 'duality and separation from Spirit' trap. When I do that, I see two sets of footprints. Every time I petition, beg, or ask an anthropomorphic God in the sky for something, I see two sets of footprints. Every time I fail to see the sacred oneness in all things, I see two sets of footprints.

"But when I remember that I am one with the One Reality, the Sacred Unity, the Great I Am, the Infinite Invisibleness—I see one distinct set of footprints. I remind myself there is no separation or duality. I remember that I am the Christ Presence expressing at the point of me! I remember the words of the Christ as Jesus when he said, 'Peace, be still.'"

© 2007 Rev. Dr. Bil Holton—This adaptation is from a metaphysical perspective. See YourSpiritualPractice.com for more metaphysical interpretations of scripture.

Life-Changing Spiritual Practices, Volume 1

Repair Rocky Roads With Forgiveness

This spiritual practice is a must! Its absence will create an impenetrable ceiling on your spiritual growth. We're not being overly dramatic. Unforgiveness is "spiritual Kryptonite." Spiritual walks without forgiveness aren't walks—they're backstrokes.

Here's How This Spiritual Practice Works:

Pick two to three rocky interpersonal relationships (these can be within your family, or outside the family circle— relatives, longtime friends, co-workers, church members, ex-husbands/wives, etc.). Review, in your own mind, the scenario leading up to the split. Spend time reflecting upon these questions:

- What factors led to your interpersonal distancing?
- What may have caused the process of disengagement, of relationship decay?
- Is there anything about the embattered relationship that has enough value in it to consider repairing it?
- In what ways do you choose to avoid contact?
- Describe the reasons behind the deterioration. What's in it for you to continue to value relation desolation over relationship repair?
- How do you feel about your own ability to manage disagreement or conflict with another spiritual being in human form? How do you raise your consciousness so you connect with the other person's Higher Self?

Study the rift. Analyze it. Place it under your intellectual and emotional microscopes. Examine every bruise, each hurtful salvo, every tear, each decision to perpetuate the adverse relationship.

Consider repairing the relationship. Start with forgiveness. What are ten things you can do to move toward a personally satisfying outcome? It may mean you've done all you can. It could mean releasing the past and moving beyond the limitations posed by such a dysfunctional relationship. However, you don't know that yet. So, make the first move. Do it! Move toward a more complete connection with the Higher Self in each of you.

© 2010 Bil and Cher Holton, YourSpiritualPractice.com

Life-Changing Spiritual Practices, Volume 1

Gardening / Landscaping

Gardening, landscaping, the tilling of the soil are the earthy extensions of our gardening, landscaping and tilling of the soil of our consciousness. Planting flowers, shrubs and trees mirrors the planting of spiritual teachings and principles in our conscious awareness. Both are natural processes. Both need tending, nurturing and growth. Both are disciplines of faith.

"Gardening is a spiritual practice. It's not about having or taking; it's about giving," says psychotherapist Gunilla Norris, author of *A Mystic Garden: Working with Soil, Attending to Soul*. "And in giving, the garden gives back to you," she adds. She is right, of course. Gardening and landscaping are two intentional paths for cultivating your spirituality.

April Thompson, in the March, 2014 edition of *Natural Awakenings* magazine, reminds us:

> We can even discover our personal calling through cultivating a garden while gleaning endless spiritual lessons: Here dwells patience and an appreciation for the natural order of things; no fertilizer can force a flower to bloom before its time. Here resides mindfulness as we learn to notice changes in the plants under our care and discern what they need to thrive. Here abides interdependence; we wouldn't have carrots, corn, or cherries without the bats, birds, and bees playing in the pollen. In a garden, we naturally accept the cycle of life, death, and rebirth as we bid adieu to the joy of seasonal colors and let flowerbeds rest in peace, anticipating their budding and blooming again. Just as the fruits of growing a garden exceed the doing—the weeding and seeding and countless other tasks—so do the riches of tending a spiritual life surpass the striving. We do well to rejoice in the sacred space created, cherishing every spiritual quality nurtured within and reflected in the Divine handiwork.

Here's How This Spiritual Practice Works:

The make-up and constitution of earthy soil and the cosmic dimensions of your consciousness are both dynamic receptacles to produce a Garden of Eden-like potentiality. Metaphysically, the Garden of Eden is your super-consciousness. It is the realm of 'divine soil' within you that spawns divine insights and ideas. It is limitless realm of possibility and expansiveness. All you have to do is grow it by keeping an open mind, move beyond dogmatic perspectives, and *feeeeeel* your oneness with your innate divinity. (You can also do some of your own gardening/landscaping as a metaphor.)

© 2001, 2003, 2014 Bil and Cher Holton, YourSpiritualPractice.com

Googling, Yahooing, Binging

*I*t is not too much of a stretch to suggest that Googling, Yahooing, and Binging can be considered apt metaphors for the ancient record of knowledge called the *Akashic Records*. The *Akashic Records* are an 'aetheric library' imprinted on an omnipresent akasha (a soniferous ether) so we can mentally 'Google' all of the past, present, and future knowledge of the universe anytime

we want, when we are in a state of heightened consciousness. Depending on our psychic sensitivity and Akashic interests, we can even 'bookmark' various knowledge banks so the information is available to us instantly because the perennial knowledge is encoded in our DNA.

These perennial records of humankind's collective mind are available to us at the level of our super-consciousness. From a technological perspective, Googling, Yahooing, and Binging serve the same purpose. They are treasure troves of the existing knowledge on the planet.

Here's How This Spiritual Practice Works:

You can Google, Yahoo, and Bing *anything* in a matter of seconds. That means you can turn these three search engines into spiritual practices by asking for spiritual content to fortify your spiritual growth. They are excellent sources for anything you want to find out about on any spiritual and/or religious subject.

Explore the benefits of these search engines. Use them as readily available tools for your spiritual growth.

© 2009, 2014 Bil and Cher Holton, YourSpiritualPractice.com

Grailology

Grailology is the spiritual practice that reinforces the metaphysical teaching that the Grail has many more meanings and attributes than a mere cup. Christ Consciousness (Buddha Consciousness, Krishna Consciousness, Great Spirit Consciousness; Vishnu Consciousness, Allah Consciousness) are all Holy Grails!

The Grail legend probably originated in Celtic and Druid traditions. The Grail's various manifestations also include, but are not limited to: the Lost Paradise, an illumined mind, a giving heart, the eternal Word of God, spiritual centers built by humankind, Arthur's Round Table, the Book of Life, the blood that flows from someone who sacrifices his/her life for others, a downward-pointing triangle, 'cupped' flowers, the calyx of a flower, the Cosmic Egg, the sacrificial cup containing the Vedic Soma, the lunar crescent, etc.

Historically there are 4 common attributes of the Grail agreed upon, but not understood, by most researchers and Grail scholars:

- The chief Grail property is that it rights the wrong of the senseless loss of an important component of our spiritual connection.
- The Grail represents the fulfillment of a grand promise which has been swept away by human greed and corruption.
- Its loss has been replaced by a wasteland of darkness where the radiance of Spirit is seldom seen or felt.
- The Grail has always been cast as a material object whose true whereabouts remains a mystery.

The first three are closer to the truth than you might think. Unfortunately, it is the fourth attribute that has gained the world's attention. It has led to expeditions throughout the world, focused on fnding this mystical vessel. In March, 2014, two historians claimed they identified the holy grail that the Christ as Jesus drank from at the last supper. León University medieval history lecturer Margarita Torres and art historian José Manuel Ortega del Rio made the claim in their book *Kings of the Grail*. Of course, crowds flocked to see the goblet of the Infanta Doña Urraca in the Basilica of San Isidoro in León, northern Spain once the historians' claim came to light. People, it seems, have a limited view of what the grail really is and are prone to settle for a physical cup or goblet.

We see it differently—hence, this spiritual practice! The Grail, in our opinion, can represent our heart, which is the somatic cup [vase] that dispenses our blood throughout our body. The Christ as Jesus' heart may also represent the Grail because it dispenses the vital force to all beings. Our physical body can also be considered the Grail because it houses our spirit as a particularization of the Eternal One. These interpretations are what make this such a powerful spiritual practice.

Here's How This Spiritual Practice Works:

This spiritual practice asks you to expand your view of the Grail, reflecting on it being an intrinsic archetype of enlightenment instead of a physical thing! Spend quality time in meditative silence, reflecting on the possible meanings of the Holy Grail, and what it could represent from a spiritual perspective.

Draw a picture illustrating your thoughts and ideas. Discover the practical use of what your perceptions could mean for you.

© 2014 Bil and Cher Holton, YourSpiritualPractice.com

"Every religion is true one way or another. It is true when understood metaphorically. But when it gets stuck in its own metaphors, interpreting them as facts, then you are in trouble,"
(Joseph Campbell)

Cultivate an Attitude of Gratitude

People who write down at least three things to be grateful for each day are happier and more optimistic than people who choose not to record what they are grateful for. And that uplifted spirit remains even after they stop recording what they were grateful for.

In this landmark study, a group of adults ranging in age from 35-54 were asked to write down each night three things that went well for them that day, and to give an explanation why. Over the next three months, their degrees of happiness continued to increase, and their feelings of depression continued to decrease, even though they had discontinued the writing experiment.

(Seligman M., Steen, T., Park, N., Peterson, C., "Positive psychology progress: empirical validation of interventions," American Psychologist, 2005 July-Aug; 60(5): 410-21).

Here's How This Spiritual Practice Works:

This spiritual practice invites you to keep a gratitude journal. Every day write down the various positive experiences that you consider as blessings ... things for which you are grateful. Then every evening before you go to sleep, say what you are grateful for out loud. You will begin seeing blessings that you weren't conscious of before, because you are focusing on positiveness instead of negativity. See the number  of blessings grow and watch your gratitude expand. Expressing your gratitude in this way usually attracts more things you can be grateful for and leaves you in a positive frame of mind just before you go to sleep.

© 2000, 2010 Bil and Cher Holton, YourSpiritualPractice.com

Eliminating Harmaceuticals

*M*edically speaking, a harmaceutical is an FDA approved medication released for public consumption by a pharmaceutical company which is recalled and becomes the subject of a class-action lawsuit because of its previously unreported dangers.

Spiritually speaking, harmaceuticals are products and information that contain some kernal of Truth, but actually share incorrect messages that can be harmful to our spiritual growth. There are lots of charletans out there who want to prey on your desire to grow spiritually, and they are more than willing to promise outlandish things in return for your money and your devotion.

Just one example is the way in which Truth Principles of Sacred Abundance and Prosperity end up promising you any material item you desire, if you only say the right affirmations and visualize in the way that particular "guru" is selling. While some of what this individual is saying is based in Truth, the focus on material goods creates a belief in some kind of magic ritual that will produce all the people, jobs, and "stuff" you ever wanted. Nothing could be farther from the Truth of Sacred Abundance Principles, which are all about an "inside-out" process.

Here's How This Spiritual Practice Works:

This spiritual practice is a good 'arrow' to keep in your spiritual growth 'quiver' because it reminds you to keep your spiratal antenna up, ready to spot any deceptive practices being sold as Truth. Test every new idea against the Truth you know.

Any new idea or practice that does not welcome your questions is not worth your time or energy. Do not walk away from people who try to force-feed some process or belief on you, no questions asked. RUN!!

Eliminate Spiritual Harmaceuticals from your life, so you can focus your time and energy on enrichment and enlightenment that is based in solid science and spiritual principles.

© 2014 Bil and Cher Holton, YourSpiritualPractice.com

Hobbies / Crafts

Find your own natural rhythm and spiritual alignment with your Higher Self by using the joy and satisfaction you feel in practicing your hobbies as a springboard to inner connection, transformation, and peace. Dip your toes into the essence of your innate divinity by dipping your mind, body, and soul into a craft or hobby.

When you have a spiritual experience, you usually feel relaxed, refreshed, centered, and peaceful. If your hobby brings out these reactions in you, then it's possible you're experiencing the spiritual benefits inherent in your hobby. Hobbies provide an escape from the sometimes monotonous nature of daily life, and they'll help you learn something about yourself in the process.

Here's How This Spiritual Practice Works:

Carve time into every week to spend focusing on your favorite hobby. If you are reading this and saying, "But I don't have a hobby," then your first step is to find one! Think about something you enjoyed doing in the past that you have let fall by the wayside. We encourage you to pick it up again. Or think about something you've been interested in, but have not taken time to explore. Delve into it now.

The possibilities are endless! Your hobby could involve crafts, sewing, art, dance. It may be photography, collectables, drawing, books, or playing music. Perhaps it focuses on landscaping, plants, bird watching, or fish. Perhaps it involves cooking, travel, sports, or writing. Try out different things and see what brings you joy.

Create a place you can dedicate to your hobby; learn more about it; connect with others who share your passion.

As you enter into the practice of hobbies and crafts, set an intention to use the time as a way to make a connection with your inner joy, your creativity, your love.

There's something about the essence of a hobby you choose that connects with 'Something' deep inside you. That 'Something' is your Divine Nature, your Authentic Self. Developing that hobby keeps you close to your Core Self. It helps ensure your alignment with your spiritual rhythm.

© 2000, 2014 Bil and Cher Holton, YourSpiritualPractice.com

Horseback Riding

Horseback riding as a spiritual practice is where "yeehaw" and "namaste" come together. Riding to improve your balance and body alignment while nurturing the horse-human connection is what this spiritual practice is all about.

The essential joy of horseback riding is that it brings you in contact with the rare elements of grace, beauty, serenity, spirit, and freedom. Many horseback riders feel their horse is somewhat of a kindred spirit in tune with their own feelings and emotions.

Horseback riding has many benefits: Cantering or galloping and jumping, for example, are much more difficult than a simple jog or trot. Riders must develop coordination skills to move their bodies with the horse. Rider's muscle tone and flexibility are enhanced. Depending on the type of riding and the speed and agility of the horse, horseback riding definitely requires more effort and energy, and has plenty of positive effects on your cardiovascular capacity.

Here's How This Spiritual Practice Works:

If you've never ridden a horse, consider this a spiritual adventure! Find a place where you can safely create the experience, and allow yourself to become one with your horse. Experience the feeling of the responsiveness that comes from your oneness with the horse's rhythm, and become aware of how the horse responds to your movements, muscle shifts, and even your thoughts.

If you are already an avid horseback rider, enter into your next ride with a conscious intention of using the experience as a spiritual practice, to become one with your Higher Self, the True You.

You will find that horseback riding, as a spiritual practice, teaches you to take one stride at a time. It can be very relaxing and invites you to 'get lost' in the scenery. It may even encourage you to 'horse around' a bit.

© 2013 Bil and Cher Holton, YourSpiritualPractice.com

iPad-ing

What on earth, you may ask, is i-Pad-ing, and what does it have to do with a spiritual practice? Well, this practice involves, of all things, your iPad or other electronic tablet.

iPad-ing, like smartphoning, can facilitate an absorbing and transformative spiritual practice. Most of the technology inherent in smartphones is available on iPads: apps, Facetiming, Internet access, messaging, Skyping, reading iBooks, etc. So, your iPad can be an excellent source for spiritual growth.

You can shoot video, take pictures, and play music on your iPad. You can queue-up its GPS navigation when you're outdoors enjoying nature, and when you want to take photos and videos, you can rotate your iPad horizontally to landscape mode. There are apps that create meditative experiences, and e-books filled with information to stretch your spiritual thinking. We are challenging you to break free from the regular ways you use your iPad or other electronic tablet, and intentionally use it as a tool for spiritual growth.

Here's How This Spiritual Practice Works:

Because you take this amazing tablet almost anywhere, you can ensure the privacy you need to use its applications for bringing you a totally absorbing spiritual experience. Look for one way each day to use your tablet as a tool to facilitate your spiritual enrichment. Pulling up music for meditations, queuing up singing bowl tones, enjoying Internet features on spiritual subjects, watching YouTubes on spirituality, taking photos and videos during spiritual outings, and so on, are all experiences you can enjoy with this versatile tool.

© 2014 Bil and Cher Holton, YourSpiritualPractice.com

Jogging

There is nothing novel about the connection between physical exercise and spirituality—it is referenced in the New Testament where the writer of I Corinthians 9:24-27 likens the training of the body to the training of the soul. Exercise in general, and jogging in particular, are recognized as disciplines of the self-denial of comfort, and are accepted ascetic practices along with fasting.

Many people do their best thinking when they jog. Ideas come, solutions sneak up on you, flashes of insight sprint into your conscious awareness. And the more you jog, the more your consciousness is flooded with thoughts to ponder.

In *Once a Runner,* John Parker expresses the feeling many of us runners have felt when he says that "running does something that nothing else does, and although at times running is difficult, it also allows us to be free and unencumbered." Jogging helps you get into the right relationship with yourself—and so does spirituality. You discover your limits are in the gray matter between your ears—and spirituality is about consciousness. When you've jogged for a while you get a 'second wind'—and in spirituality the choices you make based on faith are your 'second wind.' You learn the importance of breathing properly when you jog—and in spirituality it is the mindfulness of breathing that uses the breath as an object of concentration during meditation.

Here's How This Spiritual Practice Works:

Try jogging. If you've never done it, start small. Try to find a beautiful location to jog, such as a park, college campus, lakeside, or beach. That way, you can take in the beauty around you as you jog.

See if it is a spiritual practice that is a good fit for you. Jogging, as a spiritual practice, is not for everyone—as attested by actor and comedian Martin Mull who said, "The trouble with jogging is that the ice falls out of your glass."

© 2013 Bil and Cher Holton, YourSpiritualPractice.com

Keurig Moments

Keurig moments mean more than simply enjoying cups of Joe. They are caffeinated moments that herald peacefulness, rest, and inner satisfaction. The quirky delights of coffee life turn mere coffee cups into holy grails of pleasure.

By the way, your morning cup of coffee may taste even better after you learn that a major government study found frequent coffee drinkers have a lower risk of dying from a variety of diseases, compared with people who drink little or no coffee.

The report, published in *The New England Journal of Medicine*, analyzed the coffee-drinking habits of more than 400,000 men and women ages 50 to 71, making it the largest-ever study of the relationship between coffee consumption and health.

While coffee contains caffeine, a stimulant that may temporarily increase heart rate and blood pressure in some people, coffee also contains hundreds of unique compounds and antioxidants that may confer health benefits.

Here's How This Spiritual Practice Works:

Of course, you don't have to use a Keurig! Lots of coffee addicts prefer the act of grinding their beans, or performing the french press routine as part of their practice. The point is to transform your time with coffee into a spiritual experience. Many coffee drinkers will tell you that luxuriating in a coffee experience is like a sabbatical from daily issues and responsibilities. People hang out at cafés for hours to take a break from the daily routine and enjoy the simple experience of drinking coffee. Assuming you are a coffee drinker, turn you coffee time into a spiritual practice by giving it your total focus and attention.

Smelling the aroma from the hot cup, taking in the soothing color, relishing the rich coffee flavor, and drinking your favorite coffee are all things that mindfully help you live in the moment, feeling centered and at peace.

For some people there must be coffee before talkie! For others, robust coffee is *sacred grounds.* Still others say it is a hug in a cup. Many coffee aficionados refer to coffee as a sonnet of the senses. Others see it as a tithe to Spirit.

All coffee addicts would probably tell you that it's not procrastinating if you're enjoying a cup of coffee, it's pro-caffeinating! (All of these descriptions explain Cher's nirvanic coffee experiences—that's why we *know* Keurig moments are truly spiritual practices).

© 2014 Bil and Cher Holton, YourSpiritualPractice.com

Letting the Real You Out

This spiritual practice isn't for the 99% committed you! You've got to own your intention to grow spiritually a full 100%. One of the key connection tools is the practice of 'intensive journaling.' It is designed to capture your thoughts and experiences, and will serve as a long term recapture mechanism for sustained spiritual growth.

The uncanny value such a journal brings to your continued spiritual growth is its built-in *progressive abstraction* feature. (That is to say, it enables the well-disciplined you to progressively and systematically draw your focus on spiritual growth and enlightenment at your own tempo).

Its therapeutic value is amazing. It systematically evokes and strengthens your inner capacities by evolving from a totally subjective (and therefore subconscious) vantage point and proceeds without analytic or diagnostic categories.

Since your recorded thoughts and experiences become part of your personal journal history and are recorded systematically in your own words, you can accumulate tangible and factual validation of your personal and spiritual transformation in progress.

Here's How This Spiritual Practice Works:

Dedicate 15-30 minutes every day to writing in a personal journal. It works best if you do this at the same time every day. Just allow your thoughts to flow, and write without thinking. If you can't think of anything to write about, just let your hand go a little limp, take a deep breath and call on your guides to speak to you, and start writing! Don't worry about correct spelling, grammar, or syntax. Just write!

Do not go back and read what you have written until the end of each week. Then you get to review your thoughts from a different perspective than when you wrote. Each month, it is interesting to read through everything you've written. You will identify themes, discover a-ha's, celebrate overcoming barriers, and laugh at what seemed so difficult. You will see how your soul growth is occurring, one amazing entry at a time.

The neat psychological principle operative here is that when you are shown (in your own words) how you have reconnected with your own unfoldment, the inner thread of movement through the layers of your awareness reveals itself through your recorded insights and feelings.

This self-integrative principle, this personal thought and activity review, makes it possible for you to experience (re-experience) times of exaltation and times of despair, moments of hope and anger, crises and crossroads, successes and failures, promotions and commotions, shining moments and dull misses.

You will find that your 'intensive journal' is an unfailing boomerang (written, produced, and directed by you) which provides grist for your spiritual mill. Many people ask how long they should continue to make journal entries after they feel they have gained important insights and connected with their Higher Self. Our usual response is to invite them to make it a lifelong practice.

We believe you're worth every bit of the time and energy you devote to aligning the human you with the Authentic You. Your journal can be a 'pen and paper' journal or an electronic journal. The important thing is to begin it.

© 2010 Bil and Cher Holton, YourSpiritualPractice.com

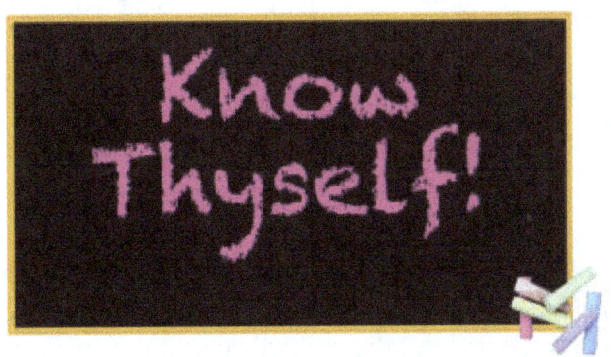

Conduct a Language Audit

Personally conduct a language audit. Listen attentively and carefully to what you say and how you say it. What labels and descriptors do you use? How positive, complementary, compassionate, and spiritual do you sound? Is your demeanor encouraging or derogatory? Does your language foul the air? Is the tone of your voice laced with negativity or thinly-disguised contempt or deceit?

Is your voice spiced with respect for others, kindness, and authentegrity? How often is your genuine—not phony—involvement expressed? Does your language express generosity and fair play? Is what you say in alignment with truth principles? Is it loving most of the time? Gentle? Angry? Fearful? Faith-oriented?

Here's How This Spiritual Practice Works:

Spend an entire week listening to your own chatter. Take mental notes. Notice the patterns and trends that emerge. Record what you hear yourself saying, especially if you say the same things a lot. What tone of voice and choice of words generally fall from your lips?

The language you use is an indicator of how connected you are to the Extraordinary You (your Higher Self). It is a barometer of disciplined practice or lukewarm practitioner. What comes out of you comes from inside of you.

We know—and you know—that once you clean up your consciousness, you'll clean up your language. Words are powerful, but they are only the effects of the consciousness behind them. Audit your language occasionally. Monitor your speech. Make sure what you say is in alignment with your current spiritual growth.

(Recommended resource to support this practice: *Get Over It! The Truth About What You Know That Just Ain't So!* and *Get Over These, Too! More Truth About What You Know That Just Ain't So!,* both by Paul Hasselbeck and Bil Holton)

© 2002, 2012 Bil and Cher Holton, YourSpiritualPractice.com

Laughing For Laughter's Sake

The truth of the matter is laughology is medicinal. And it's a great spiritual practice to adopt for that reason if nothing else. Norman Cousins, longtime editor of *Saturday Review*, learned this during a battle with a debilitating illness. He discovered that his condition improved when he enjoyed himself and watched funny movies. "Laughing," he wrote, "is like inner jogging. It helps us heal by activating the immune system." Many sick people have taken his advice and incorporated humor into their recovery regimen by watching comedies or reading collections of jokes.

A good belly laugh is infectious. And everything from a slight giggle to a side-splitting guffaw can change the 'temperature' in a room from chilly unfamiliarity to a warm family-like atmosphere.

What's more, the sound of roaring laughter is much more contagious than any cough, sniffle, or sneeze. When laughter is shared, it binds people together by elevating their level of comfort with each other and increasing the trust they feel. Laughter triggers healthy physical and emotional changes in the body. Humor and laughter strengthen the immune system by activating our T cells, boosting our energy, diminishing pain, helping us keep a positive outlook, and protecting our heart from the damaging effects of stress. Best of all, this priceless, medicinal spiritual practice is fun, free, and easy to use.

Laughter comes straight from the depths of our soul. As mentioned above, a good laugh has scientifically proven benefits and gives more oxygen to our body to remain healthy. The funny bone is in our DNA. So, appreciate your built-in ability to laugh.

Although Laughter Clubs are ideal platforms to cultivate this playfulness, you can develop a laughter spiritual practice on your own, too. There is no one proper way of laughing. You can develop your own comfort zone by using different sounds, gestures, and postures to facilitate your laughing alone. Because everyone is different, it is important that you create your own exercises and develop new ideas to discover what works best for you.

Here's How This Spiritual Practice Works:

You can begin with a brief 30 seconds of laughing time, and gradually increase the duration of your laugh-athon. Laughter, as a spiritual practice, can be scheduled for any time during the day and for as many times as you want. A good time to start is the first thing in the morning because it will carry the cheerful mood and good feelings right through the day.

If you don't feel like laughing early in the morning, begin with some warming up exercises like Ho Ho-ing and Ha Ha-ing, talking gibberish, thinking about something funny, and so on. You can also make different sounds of laughter like 'Ha ha ha, Hee hee hee, Ho ho ho' for a few minutes. It's a bit silly, of course. But you'll find that you'll start laughing genuinely at hearing the absurd sounds of your own laughter.

Once you get yourself going, take a long breath and start saying Haaaa Haaaa Haaaa Haaaa Haaaa, five to seven times. Then try to laugh and keep laughing until you run out of breath. Do your best to keep the sound of Haaaaa Haaaaa within the same breath so you empty your lungs out completely. In the beginning it might feel a bit awkward, but your bouts of real laughter will come.

You will notice from our description so far that we are encouraging you to build a laughter practice into your day as both a medicinal and spiritual practice exercise. You can find humor in magazines, TV shows, YouTubes, and conversations with friends—and those outlets are fine. Laughter, as we've mentioned before, is medicinal.

However, the purpose of a spiritual practice that focuses on laughter is to get you to, well, laugh! Laughter clubs, get-togethers with friends and family, and joke books are aspects of your laughology practice, but it's important to laugh at other times as well to make laughter a habit. (And every now and then, it's a good practice to look at yourself in the mirror and laugh! Try it ... you'll see what we mean!)

© 2002, 2010 Bil and Cher Holton, YourSpiritualPractice.com

Laughter is an instant vacation.
(Milton Berle)

Soulful Music

Music is an incredible tool to use as a spiritual practice, and there are a multitude of ways it can be done. This is one practice that is designed to use music as a mood-setting, emotion-settling backdrop to your contemplative time.

Here's How This Spiritual Practice Works:

Let's start with some tips on choosing the appropriate music:

- Select music that is soothing and calming, and which appeals to your musical preferences.
- It is best to use instrumental music that is lyrical, rather than actual tunes to songs you know.
- Genres such as Relaxation, Nature, Classical, and Instrumental often contain excellent selections.
- Try several different artists to explore the various ways different types of music impact your inner focus results.

Set up your music so all you need to do is start it when you are ready.

Then find a comfortable sitting position that you can hold for 10-15 uninterrupted minutes. Take a few deep breaths, exhaling slowly between each. Without trying to force your breathing in any way, allow yourself to find your own natural depth and rhythm.

Start your music, and give your full attention to the coming and going of your breath. As you begin to notice a regular, slow breathing pattern, listen to the music. Pay attention to the sounds as they unfold. Let yourself become totally enveloped by the music you have chosen.

If you realize your mind has wandered off, and you find yourself engrossed in planning or day-dreaming, simply acknowledge it, then gently but firmly bring your attention back to the music.

Continue this process throughout your contemplative time. When the music has ended, or your centering session is complete, take a few deep breaths, and slowly become aware of your surroundings. Then take a few minutes to record your experience and/or your thoughts and intuitions in your Journal.

© 2000, 2012 Bil and Cher Holton, YourSpiritualPractice.com

Life-Changing Spiritual Practices, Volume 1

Multiple Listings

*P*rofessionally, we use lists as time management tools. Personally, we use them to remind us of the things we need to do, buy, or keep track of so we don't forget. We call them "To-Do Lists." Spiritually, they may serve the same purpose as we outlined above, but the focus is not as mundane as personal and professional to-dos.

The multiple listings we propose in this spiritual practice will help you organize your thoughts around important personal and spiritual themes. They will help you uncover proclivities toward health, wealth, and wellness; crystallize core values and spiritual beliefs; lasso long-forgotten experiences; spawn life-enriching insights; identify self-actualizing tendencies; magnify attitudes and assumptions; unzip memories; immortalize successes and italicize failures; revisit old patterns; and focus on defining the real you, the updated you, the you that's moving toward aligning your human self with your Higher Self.

The self-definitional lists on the next few pages are designed to help you integrate your beliefs, attitudes, and experiences and achieve the connection with your Authentic Self. You'll be asked to get beneath the surface on key spiritual life issues ... to get past the obvious.

Here's How This Spiritual Practice Works:

This is an on-going practice that covers an entire year—so get ready for some intense experiences! You'll need a notebook, pen or pencil, or computer. Check out our "Multiple Listings" beginning on the next page, and select one of the lists as a starting point. Each week for the next 52 weeks, generate 24 responses for the particular list you've chosen for that week. Try to create the list in one or two sittings over the course of the same day. (We know. It's a bit laborious, but you'll be glad you did). And of course, you can add items throughout the week, too. You can go over 24 if you want, too. No one is standing over you with a big stick!

The sheer volume of entries will dredge up life-changing information from your subconscious mind. Be sure to complete each list as fully as possible. We're not talking about ten or fifteen items—the goal is a *minimum* of 24 for each topic. That's a Double Dozen! (We know—this sounds hard! But as Tom Hanks said in *A League of Their Own*, "If it wasn't hard, everyone would do it! The hard ... is what makes it great!")

After you've completed the list, review it with an eye toward themes. Use whatever taxonomy you want to classify the entries into categories or themes. Spend the rest of the week in contemplation, allowing insights to come.

Ask yourself penetrating questions such as: What have I learned from this list that will help me become the best Divine Being I can be? A more mature person? Enrich my thinking? Create positive changes in my life? Identify my strengths? Expose my weaknesses? What would the top three priorities be for each list? How can I learn from mistakes? In what ways can I celebrate my spiritual progress? What personal, professional, and spiritual goals will I establish immediately to improve the alignment between my human self and my True Self?

Internalize what you have learned. Choose to be deepened by this provocative and highly introspective spiritual practice. Move toward a richer and fuller, more connected Authentic You.

Multiple Listings

Each of the following lists is recommended as an introspective growing edge. Spend quality time on each list, as you create your Double Dozen responses, and then reflect on what these responses have to tell you. Start anywhere, but be sure to complete all 52 Multiple Listings.

Things I Believe In
Things I Do Well
Things I'd Like to Know More About
Things I Could Learn From Children
Things I Could Learn From Nature
Reasons to Grow Spiritually
Accomplishments I'm Proud Of
Things I'd Do If I Had Time
Truth Principles I Want to Know More About
Things I'm Grateful For
Ways I Sabotage My Success
Things That Are Going Right
Things That I Allow To Derail Me
Things That Once Frightened Me, But Don't Anymore
Benefits of Disciplined Meditation
Things I've Done Before (But Haven't Done in a While) That
    I'd Like To Do Again
Sacrifices I've Made
Lessons I've Learned In Life
Ways I Can Make Money
Concerns About Being Wealthy and Healthy
Ways I Support Others
Material Things I Value
Things That Really Motivate Me
Talents, Skills, and Abilities I Have

Life-Changing Spiritual Practices, Volume 1

Books That Have Been Especially Meaningful To Me
Talents, Skills, and Abilities I Wish I Had
Extraordinary Ordinary People Who Have Died
Famous People I'd Like To Meet
Things I'd Take With Me To The Moon
Things I Haven't Finished
Things I'll Never Do Again
Ways I'm Generous
Things That Have Made Me Shed A Few Tears
Possessions I'm Tired Of Owning
Responsibilities I'd Like to Avoid
Things That Make Me Laugh/Smile
Ways I'm Selfish
Things I Get Excited About
Places I'd Like To Visit/Live
Rules I've Broken
Historical Events I'd Like To Know More About
Things All Of The World's Religions Have In Common
Ways I Could Improve Myself
Contributions I Could Make To The World
Adjectives I Could Use To Describe Myself
Things I'd Do If I Could Take A Year Off Of Work
Decisions Other People Have Made For Me
Places I Wouldn't Want To Visit
Foods I'm Eating That Make My Physical Body A Good Temple For My Extraordinary Self
Ways Forgiveness Can Transform The World
Reasons To Love My Neighbor
Ways These Multiple Listings Have Changed My Life

© 2003, 2007 Bil and Cher Holton, YourSpiritualPractice.com

Omvana

Om or Aum is an Eastern mantra and mystical sound of Hindu origin, used as a sacred incantation used at the beginning and end of a reading or prior to any prayer or mantra. The Sanskrit name for the syllable is *praṇava*, from the root *nu* 'to shout, sound, or make a humming or droning sound.'

The word Aum consists of three sounds: a (a-kāra), u (u-kāra), and m (ma-kāra). *A-kara* means 'form or shape' like the earth, trees, or any other object. *U-kāra* means 'formless or shapeless' like water, air or fire. *Ma-kāra* means 'neither shape nor shapeless (but still exists)' like dark matter in the Universe.

The syllable 'Om' describes the *All-Encompassing Mystical Consciousness* that started creation with an original vibration manifesting as the sound 'OM.' It is the manifestation of God, the Eternal Presence, in physicality. It is believed to be the basic sound of the world and to contain all other sounds. When taken letter by letter, A-U-M represents the divine energy (*Shakti*) united in its three elementary aspects: *Brahma Shakti* (creation), *Vishnu Shakti* (preservation) and *Shiva Shakti* (liberation, and/or destruction).

Repeating the '*Oṃ maṇi padme hūṃ*' as a spiritual practice is a well-known six-syllabled Sanskrit mantra. *Mani* means 'jewel' or 'bead' and *Padma* means 'lotus flower, which is the Buddhist sacred flower. Our favorite translation is: *Om* purifies bliss and pride (realm of the gods); *Ma* purifies jealousy and need for self-aggrandizing entertainment (realm of the jealous gods); *Ni* purifies passion and desire (realm of human wants); *Pad* purifies ignorance and prejudice (realm of animal instincts); *Me* purifies selfishness and possessiveness (realm of the hungry ghosts); *Hum* purifies aggression and hatred (realm of a hellish state of consciousness).

The 14th Dalai Lama, Lhamo Dondrub, sums it up this way: "The six syllables, *om mani padme hum*, mean that in dependence on the practice of a path which is an indivisible union of method and wisdom, you can transform your impure body, speech, and mind into the pure exalted body, speech, and mind of a Buddha,"

Neuroscientists agree that affirmations repeated often enough change our brain chemistry: "The mere repetition of a sound or phrase over a period of time significantly reduces symptoms of stress, anxiety, depression, and anger, while improving the practitioner's perception of the quality of life and spiritual well-being." *(R. Spencer, T. Verstynen, M. Brett, and R. Ivry, "Cerebellar activation during discrete and not continuous timed movements: An fMRI study," Neuroimage, 2007, June, 36 (2): 378-87).*

According to the Mandukya Upanishad, "*Om* is the one eternal syllable of which all that exists is but the continued development of it. The past, the present, and the future are all infolded in this one sound, and all that exists is implied in it."

Here's How This Spiritual Practice Works:

Find a comfortable position where you will be uninterrupted for 30 minutes. Practice some deep breathing to bring yourself to a centered, quiet state. Then begin intoning the word *Om,* keeping the word above your breath, even and peaceful. Allow yourself to feel the gentle vibration of your lips, as they close around the end of the word, and sense the energy flow as you continue holding the vibration on the "m" sound. As your breath ends, inhale again, and repeat the process.

If repeated with the correct intonation, the power of *Om* can resonate throughout your body so that the sound penetrates to the center of your being, your Authentic Self. This is the state of trance, where the mind and the intellect are transcended as your human self merges with the Infinite Self in the pious moment of Self realization. It is a moment when petty worldly affairs are lost in the desire for universal oneness.

© 2002 Bil and Cher Holton, YourSpiritualPractice.com

An In-Depth Reading:
Don't Suffer From a Pain in the Ask

Two lawyers were on their way back to their car from the Dean Center when they were stopped by an armed robber.

"Your money and your watches or your lives," he sneered, pointing his handgun at them.

"May I have a moment, please?" asked one of the victims. The puzzled robber gave his consent, but steadied his gaze and gun on both of them.

The woman took off her watch and reached into her purse, taking out $300 dollars and handed it to her companion.

"Here's the money I owe you,' she said. "We're all square now!"

Her timing was impeccable. Her creativity and quick thinking helped her pay off a creditor. All because she didn't suffer from a pain in the ask!

Although this story is amusing, it makes a very important point: Most people ask for too little instead of too much. The kind of asking we're referring to is not a verb but an acronym. We'll explain what the acronym means in a few moments, after we share what 'asking' isn't.

In Matthew 21:22 the Christ as Jesus said: "Whatever we ask for in prayer, believing with faith, we shall receive." (By the way, the word "Ask" is a mistranslation. In the original Aramaic, the word means declare or affirm.) This simple passage reflects a simple truth. But it is one of the most powerful teachings of Jesus.

Most people have been taught by the faith traditions in which they grew up to ask, to petition, to beg an external anthropomorphic deity for something they believe they don't have. They use ask as a verb to hopefully win the favor of a God who plays favorites.

As Unity ministers we take another position. We do not believe we are separate from God. We believe we are the human expressions of God in human form. For us, ask takes on a whole different meaning. We "ask" from an awareness of our Oneness. In other words, we declare our good. We affirm our good. We take the position that asking in the form of a verb reinforces the falsehood that we are separate from Spirit. We have turned ASK into an acronym:

Affirm it • **S**ee it • **K**now it.

In the world of martial arts, asking is more acronym than verb too. In Bil's past life (a 'past life' in this life), when he was in his 30's, he was a student of karate. (He actually did it to accompany our son, who was about 8 at the time, and Cher went too. But she did not like the Sensai walking on her stomach! And her nails got in the way of knuckle push ups!) Anyway, to move on with the story ... Whenever students were ready to be tested for their next higher belt, they asked for it! Not the verb ask but the acronym ask. Here's how it worked:

When the students thought they were ready to test for their next belt, the Sensai scheduled the test. All of the students who had earned higher belts, including those who possessed the belt the student was testing for, stood in a line in order of their respective belts. The student would walk along the line, from the lower belts to the higher belts, and stop in front of the person h/she chose to test his/her karate skills. They *asked*, that is they *declared* their readiness to be tested in combat. No words were spoken. The idea was to let their actions prove their readiness.

In the 'real' world, our actions prove our readiness too. We ask, that is, we declare, we **affirm** from the consciousness that, at the level of Spirit, we already have what we want at the human level of our being. All we have to do is affirm prayerfully, believing, and we shall demonstrate the connection.

We'd like to share a true story which demonstrates the power of not suffering from a pain in the ask:

> Len LeSourd began working for a magazine just before Thanksgiving Day in 1946. He eventually became the magazine's Editor-in-Chief for over 25 years. Two months after he started work, a fire from a defective chimney burned the business down. Everything, including the subscriber files, was destroyed.
>
> One of the Board Members of the magazine was Lowell Thomas, who went on the air and told of the plight of the magazine and of the lost subscriber data base. Letters poured in from subscribers and new orders as well, doubling the circulation. Things happened so quickly that they couldn't meet the demand—or pay the expenses that had accumulated with the purchase of a new building and equipment.
>
> By the summer of 1948 the magazine was $32,000 in debt. Their printer refused to print another press run. Publication stopped.
>
> Len's father knew an elderly, wealthy Jewish woman—Tessie Durlack who might be able to help. When Len, his father, and the Publisher called on her at her elegant Park Avenue apartment, the first thing she said was, "Let's pray about it." And then she said, "We must ask for divine ideas and direction."
>
> "Next," she continued, "We must wait and listen. When we hear something, we must write it down, no matter how strange or irrelevant it seems."
>
> The magazine's Publisher, Board, and Len did as she said. After 45 minutes of silence, with the only sounds being the scratching of pens on paper as people jotted down any thoughts they "heard," she asked them to read what they had recorded.

Len was the first to speak. He apologized to the group and then read his first entry: "I need a haircut."

Everyone but Tessie was dumbfounded. "That's great," she shouted, "You are priming the pump."

After Len finished sharing the rest of his list, and the others added their input, Tessie rose to her feet and said, "You have a big problem here. You run this business from a lack mentality. All I've heard is what you don't have. You are never going to succeed unless you learn to be more positive. You have to learn to picture in your minds and declare confidently what you want this magazine to be! And Len, I believe your 'haircut' insight means this company needs to cut negativity out of your heads."

"And to help you see that," she continued, "I'm going to write you a check for $5,000 to get you started."

And the rest, as they say, is history. The magazine, *Guideposts,* is still in circulation today, thriving and growing.

By the way, one of the outcomes of Tessie's 'come to Jesus' session was the inspiration of one of the best selling books of all time. As a direct result of that session, one of the people attending, Rev. Norman Vincent Peale, went home and started writing *The Power of Positive Thinking!*

The power of seeing ask as an acronym and not a verb will make a huge difference—all the difference—in your life!

How many times have you read Matthew 21:22 (Ask, believing you have received) and said, "Yeah, right! I've asked, but it's not coming. So this verse just isn't true!" Actually, this verse is a kind of mystery and the clue is in the very word giving us the problem: ASK. As we mentioned before, "Ask" should really be interpreted as "Declare."

From this perspective, an example would be asking the spigot for water, or asking the wall outlet for light, We may not understand the specifics of how the principles of running water or electricity work, but we know they are principles we depend on. We don't go up to the sink, get on our knees, and beg for water. We simply "work the principle!"

In our work, we have long used this phrase as one of our basic principles for success: *Don't suffer from a pain in the Ask!* Do you realize how fearful people are of asking?

So what does that have to do with our receiving all we ask for? What does it mean to ask, believing we have received? To understand that, you need to read between the lines, and see the word ASK as a word that holds three clues to how we are to Declare: Affirm • See • Know.

Life-Changing Spiritual Practices, Volume 1

Here's How This Spiritual Practice Works:

AFFIRM: Affirm something you desire by speaking as if it is already a done deal … from a consciousness of abundance rather than from a consciousness of lack. Listen to the words you speak. They will tell you where your consciousness is! Are you focused on what you don't have? Make the mental shift to affirming what it is you are seeking. Say it in positive terms, and say it with confidence and energy!

Affirming your requests transforms your magnetic field, so you actually begin aligning your human self with your Higher Self so your prosperity can manifest through you. Now here's a little secret: instead of affirming a specific outcome, try affirming the essence of what you want. (For example, instead of affirming that you get a raise, affirm that you are financially free, with all your bills paid and plenty to share and spare. Instead of, "I no longer suffer from asthma," affirm "I have now transcended all patterns of illness. I am free and healthy!").

SEE: Visualize yourself embodying the essence of what it is you are affirming. Visualizing is often misunderstood, because not everyone sees in mental pictures. There are many ways to "visualize" or "see" what you are declaring.

KNOW: Know that knowing comes from deep within—where you know that you know that you know! It is the knowing that allows you to simply turn the faucet to get water—to hit the switch knowing you will get light. Imagine if we had that same kind of belief about our spirituality!

> *There's a classic clinical story we still remember learning about years ago in a Clinical Psychology course. The story is of a young man who suddenly believes he is dead—a walking corpse. His exasperated parents struggle with him, and finally arrange an appointment with a highly respected New York City psychiatrist. The psychiatrist tried his professional best to convince the young man that he was not a corpse, and that he was certainly not dead.*
>
> *The two men fruitlessly argued the point back and forth. Finally the psychiatrist had an idea he was certain would convince the young man that his belief was erroneous. The psychiatrist turned to the young man and asked, "Do you think dead people bleed?" The young man thought about this for a moment, then answered: "No, all body functions have stopped when you're dead. So there would be no blood flowing."*
>
> *The psychiatrist then took a needle from his desk and pricked the young man's finger. The young man gasped and stared at his finger in amazement. "Well," he finally stammered. "I'll be darned. Dead people DO bleed!" His belief was so powerful that logical evidence had no influence over it at all.*

Life-Changing Spiritual Practices, Volume 1

So, **Affirm it—See it—Know it**— believing you have received. The Christ as Jesus taught us and demonstrated the power of declaring from this consciousness, with His miracles, and His healings. We can do what He did, once we know the secret of the word ASK. Affirm it, See it, and Know that you know that you know that your good comes through you! Then pay attention, listen, and act. We guarantee that from this 'declarative' consciousness, you truly can ask, believing you have received, and it will be yours!

© 1989, 2006, 2013 Bil and Cher Holton, *YourSpiritualPractice.com*

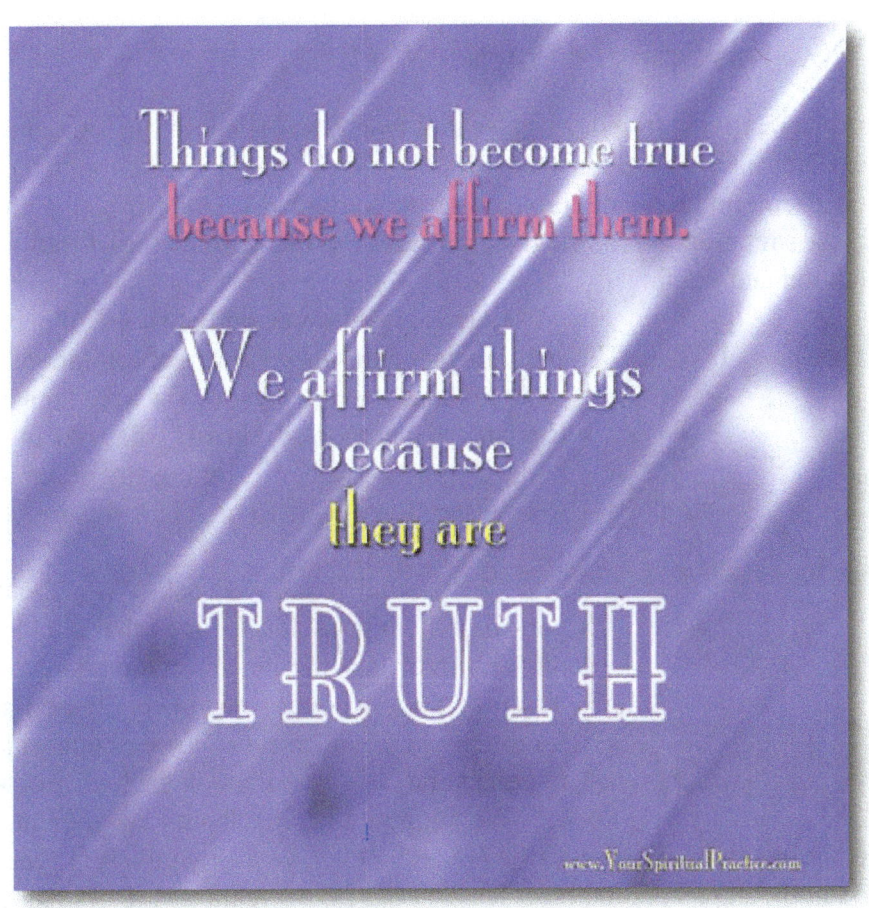

Rendezvous With Your Past, Present and Future

With sober and serious introspection, write your autobiography. No doubt this will be an exacting task, for self-exploration is as much self-recovery as it is self-discovery. The review process is a sobering one. It calls for a serious attempt to make your individualization process a conscious journey. Sustained investigation and serious reflection are necessary prerequisites for just the right amount of psychic material to percolate up into your conscious awareness.

Here's How This Spiritual Practice Works:

Interview relatives, friends, high school teachers, college professors and classmates, co-workers. Revisit old neighborhoods (if possible). Connect yourself with the past. Spend a nostalgic afternoon browsing through old photographs. Take a trip to the attic—dust off the old chest—reminisce. Collide head-on with the old you. Descend into the depths of your childhood and youth.

Excavate your own toddler shoes, or baby blanket, or first finger painting. Resurrect childhood memories, realizing that was the person you were then and not now. Revisit old yearbooks. Unpack that old high school or college sports sweater. Admire memorabilia. Reflect. Reminisce. Recollect. Remember. Resurrect. Then start writing.

"Write what?" you may ask. Write about the you of your past—thoughts and feelings that bubble up; images that resurrect, and the meaning you attach to them now. You may even uncover some deeply buried hurts or long forgotten cherished events. Write about whatever flows to your mind, as you reflect on each year of your past.

We suggest that the length of your autobiography should be not less than one type-written page for each year of your age. If you're 41 years old, your autobiography should be at least 41 pages; 55 years young, 55 pages of text; 93 years young, 93 pages long.

Spend quality time on this spiritual practice. Your personal and spiritual evolution and unfoldment have brought you to where you are today. Each day is a launch site for tomorrow. Your well-researched life review will be a springboard for the new you, the Authentic You, the SuperSelf™ You.

Life-Changing Spiritual Practices, Volume 1

Our hope is that you will proceed faithfully from the first page to the last. That you will emerge not only with a substantial understanding and appreciation of where you've been, but also with a revitalized psyche and renewed interest in introspection, self-evaluation, and self-definition ... Because you are a constellation of experience ... A spiritual being having a human experience ... One who is successfully matriculating through this multi-curriculumed classroom we call skin school.

The difference between your natural unfoldment, which runs its course unconsciously, and the one which is consciously realized, is tremendous. The therapeutic effects are lasting. The self-integration transforming. So, go ahead. Do it now. Rendezvous with your past, present, and future by taking a backward glance (ecnalg), a present look, and a future peek.

© 2001, 2008, 2014 Bil and Cher Holton, YourSpiritualPractice.com

Peace Vigil

A peace vigil is a way of expressing your commitment for world peace. Peace vigils do not—in and of themselves—stop wars or transform the nature of violence. They are valuable as personal demonstrations of a commitment to peace that advocates a worldwide culture of peace.

Your peace vigil creates a pocket of awareness that advocates peace. It represents your intention to show that peace is possible. It communicates a peace message to the universe that you are an advocate for peace.

Your intentionality adds to the consciousness of others opposing war and violence, and legitimizes the quest for peace. It demonstrates your belief that peace can be accomplished with courage, compassion, and conviction. It transforms your vigil into a global vigil for peace that has local roots.

It unites your individual dedication with people all over the world by forming a community of shared purpose.

This spiritual practice can be very fulfilling as an avenue for you to express your spirituality in a private way that has global implications.

Here's How This Spiritual Practice Works:

Spend a block of time in the Silence, focusing on peace. Imagine the essence of peace flowing from your heart center out into the world, touching every single person, bringing harmony and peace. Hear Mother Earth say "Thank You!"

© 2000 Bil and Cher Holton, YourSpiritualPractice

Life-Changing Spiritual Practices, Volume 1

Enjoying the Performing Arts

Conversations with performing artists and exposure to new creative works have increasingly made apparent to us the significant role spirituality plays in the artist's private experience and the artistic process. The spirituality of the artists affects and determines the imagery and forms of what they create.

In their journal article, *Art as a Spiritual Practice,* the authors* report: "A cursory  overview of avant-garde and modernist movements, beginning in the late-nineteenth century, reveals the extent to which much of the most advanced performing arts drew on religious iconography, biblical themes, lives of saints, the occult, and deep spiritual feelings, joining Western, Asian, and Middle Eastern religious traditions. Alongside the impact, in the last half-century, of Buddhism and Judaism, and Catholicism, there has been growing attention to the spiritual styles of artworks."

You can enrich your spiritual experience by creating opportunities to enjoy the performing arts. It makes an incredible spiritual practice!

Here's How This Spiritual Practice Works:

Schedule an opportunity to attend a presentation involving one of the performing arts (i.e., theatre, ballet, ballroom and other dance forms, mime, magic, etc.), with the intent of allowing the movement and emotion of the performance to flow into your deepest being, touching your heart and soul. Without judgment of the performers' abilities, let their emotion and message through movement speak to you. Chat with them following the performance, if possible, to gain insight into their motivation for what they do.

When you leave the performance, set aside time to meditate on the experience, and journal your thoughts. Whichever of the performing arts you choose to adopt as a spiritual practice, you will come to know that the performing arts vibrate out of the soul as a pulse of life asking Spirit to take physical form. The tapestry of a particular performing art form is woven into the rhythm of your being. It has been there all along. Fundamental to your human expression is the language of your spirituality and sacredness.

The performing arts are concerned with being deeply alive and present in your natural artistry. They are the physical and emotional 'spaces' where you can connect with that 'Something' inside of you that is the Essential You, your Authentic Self.

*Alison Knowles, Eleanor Heartney, Meredith Monk, Linda Montano, Erik Ehn, and Bonnie Marranca

© 2014 Bil and Cher Holton, YourSpiritualPractice.com

Philanthropy

*A*n open palm instead of a closed fist is the conceptual foundation for this important spiritual practice. We're going to toss two questions at you as attention getters:

- Is your consciousness filled with pockets of resistance or pockets of plenty?
- Are your motives lined with self-interest or filled with a sense of philanthropy?

We hope these opening questions gave you a moment of pause, because they are central to the essence of this spiritual practice. And a giving consciousness is critical for your connecting with your Core Essence.

Your personal and professional success and happiness are never more than a thought or act of generosity away! Your success, as one who champions generosity, is closer than the objects which appear in your rearview mirror. It's as close as your next breath. It's as close as your next thought, intention, or choice. It's as close as your willingness to give generously and often to others.

We're going to mention one of a number of scientific findings that reinforces the value of a giving consciousness: Neurobiologically speaking, a giving consciousness is nestled within the same frontal regions of the brain which are activated by awe, wonder, transcendence, and joy. An internal coherence results, which fortifies your immune system, strengthens the neural pathways in the frontal lobe, and arrests the feelings of fear and uncertainty which are the products of the amygdala.

Gratefulness is one of your deepest connections to your Core Essence. It acknowledges your oneness with and appreciation for the Authentic You. It is the realization that there is more to you than the circumstances you face. It is the recognition that you have a capacity to give that outshines any thoughts of lack.

Here's How This Spiritual Practice Works:

Look for opportunities to give! It doesn't matter how much, or what you are giving. This spiritual practice is all about the intention of giving. People who routinely practice generosity enjoy higher levels of positivity; are more alert, alive and awake; are more joyful, express more optimism and happiness; are more helpful, generous and compassionate; are more forgiving and more outgoing; and tend to feel less lonely and isolated.

A giving consciousness seems to be an Rx for the whole body. And it's also the royal road to connecting with what neuroscientists call your Deeper Self, and what we refer to as the Extraordinary You, your Higher Self.

© 2000 Bil and Cher Holton, YourSpiritualPractice.com

Still Photography

What if every time you picked up a camera, you thought of this tool as a means for revealing the sacredness and value of life? The spiritual practice of photography can serve as a rich vehicle for deepening your way of seeing, being, appreciating and revealing the ever-present soul essence in everything through a divine projector called a camera.

Viewing the world through a camera lens gives you an opportunity to select objects that are part of the whole. This frame-by-frame awareness of the world you live in allows you to truly see—*feeeeel*—and then reveal the sacred, lifting your consciousness from an ordinary awareness to a truly extraordinary awareness of the interrelationship of things. If you've ever seen the still photography of our friend and colleague Dewitt Jones, you'll agree how spiritual stills can be. (Google Dewitt Jones on YouTube to see what we're talking about!)

If you approach photography as a spiritual practice with reverence and intention, it can help you to see holy moments all around you. In this sacred practice you are invited to take your camera out into the world each week for photo-ops that can turn into spiritual journeys. You'll find yourself cultivating sacred seeing, which is your ability to see beneath the world of appearances. You will begin to see things differently, and in the images that beckon to you, you will discover aspects of yourself that are in alignment with your own innate divinity.

Photography as a spiritual practice is visual and kinesthetic, personally enriching and soul deepening, a vehicle of self-expression and self-discovery. It is about cultivating your ability to see with the 'eyes of the heart' (Ephesians 1:18). In spiritual and mystical traditions, the heart is the seat of the soul. To "see with the heart" means you bring your whole essence to whatever reality you find in the images you capture on film.

Here's How This Spiritual Practice Works:

Grab a camera—even your smartphone will work. Take a walk anywhere, and begin to capture snapshots of what you see. Look for unusual perspectives—different points of view. Have fun transforming your environment into photographs.

Download your photos, and use them to create inspiration for your meditation time. See if any of them stimulate a desire to write stories. Post them on social media to share with others.

Consider photography as a spiritual practice so you can capture the sacred in the ordinary. You will be surprised at how much of the 'spiritual you' comes out.

© 2005 Bil and Cher Holton, YourSpiritualPractice.com

Time Lapse Photography

One of the most beautiful, mesmerizing, and inspiring spiritual practices is watching time lapse photography. Still photography is a wonderful spiritual practice, too, as we've just shared—but time lapse photography is still photography in stunning motion!

If you've ever seen Louie Schwartzberg's time lapse photography brilliance, you'll agree! He is an award-winning cinematographer, director, and producer who captures breathtaking images of nature that celebrate life—revealing the spiritual connections, universal harmony and rhythms, patterns and beauty that we share with nature. The filmmaker explains the spiritual side of what he captures on film this way:

"Metamorphosis has always been the greatest symbol of change for poets and artists. Imagine that you could be a caterpillar one moment and a butterfly the next."

In that sage statement, Louie truly captures what every spiritual practice is all about: seeing the connection between our human self (caterpillar) and our Christ Self (butterfly). And as a spiritual medium, time lapse photography focuses our attention on the continuity of our spiritual journey as we unfold into the innate divinity that is our birthright as spiritual beings having a human experience.

Here's How This Spiritual Practice Works:

Google the phrase "time lapse photography" or Louis Schwartzberg. Either search will bring up beautiful examples of time lapse photography. Louis Schwartzberg even has a few Ted Talks, where he explains his process and what it means.

Immerse yourself in this medium. Spend a chunk of quality time watching the incredible visuals and stunning images as they merge into each other. Let them speak to your soul, and then journal about your experience.

Use this spiritual practice as a way to escape from the hectic pace of your life, and experience the divine order of the unfoldment of the world in front of your eyes. You will emerge a stronger, more peaceful, more awakened person as a result.

© 2014 Bil and Cher Holton, YourSpiritualPractice.com

A Penny for Your Positive Thoughts

*M*ost people are surprised at how negative they really are. They think negatively, talk negatively, refer to themselves and others negatively, and generally negate anything that comes into their sphere of awareness.

Psychologists tell us that most of us grew up in negative environments—home, school, church, work, etc. Neuroscientists even have a word for it. It's called the "negativity bias."

Some people have Ph.D.'s in negativity. Don't you agree? You probably know some of them. There are people who wear negativity like a badge of honor. Others wear it like a straight jacket and struggle to get themselves out of a negative disposition. Negativity comes from a consciousness grounded in lack, and fear, and anger, and hopelessness.

Here's the thing. All of us have been exposed to negative environments. We've been told we're not good enough, that we're failures, that we can't do certain things or have certain things. And there's a part of us, that wounded child part of us, that says—what if they're right? We put a positive spin on that kind of malpractice by saying—negation is simply a choice you don't have to make. And you certainly don't have to allow it to form outposts in your consciousness.

So, it's important to become aware of how often you think, say, and act positively. And that's what this spiritual practice is all about. It is designed to help you focus on a positive mindset.

Here's How This Spiritual Practice Works:

Find some sort of clear plastic bottle (bank, bowl, container) in which you can collect pennies. We're suggesting that you select a clear container so you can see the amount of pennies the container holds.

Carry an index card, Post-It-Note, or slip of paper with you. (Keep it in your pocket, wallet, or purse). Be aware of each time you have a positive thought, feeling, word, or action. Do your best to acknowledge your positiveness by recording a hash mark on the Post-It-Note (slip of paper, index card) as soon possible after you become aware of it.

At the end of the day, count the number of hash marks which 'prove' how positive you've been all day. Place a penny for each hash mark in your bank (bottle, container). Watch the pennies "grow" during the course of the week. (Although you won't see your newly formed neurons growing in your brain, neuroscientists assure us that positive thoughts and actions add new neural real estate and strengthen our neural connections. It's called neuroplasticity).

Life-Changing Spiritual Practices, Volume 1

At the end of the week empty the container (bank, bottle) and put the pennies in bank coin wrappers. It's beginning to look like a mini savings account, right? Save the full penny rolls to deposit in the bank (when you accumulate a sufficient number of rolls).

Putting your 'banking' aside, the pennies will become visible evidence of your positive outlook on life. They'll symbolize your growing positivity quotient. Focusing on positive thoughts limits negative thoughts—the negative thoughts are crowded out. When you keep negative thoughts from intruding, you begin to re-program your neural real estate by strengthening the neural pathways toward a "positivity bias!" And that's the direction you want to go to align your human self with your SuperSelf™, your Christ Self, the Extraordinary You.

Repeat this spiritual practice as often as you can, as a way of checking up on yourself and reinforcing your personal positivity.

© 2000, 2013 Bil and Cher Holton, YourSpiritualPractice.com

Pinteresting

You would be surprised at how valuable and spiritually deepening Pinteresting can be as a spiritual practice. It is an online visual connection tool that people use to post their ideas and interests. You can create and share collections (pinboards) of visual bookmarks (pins). Pinterest allows you to save images and categorize them on different boards. You can follow other users' boards if they have similar interests as yours.

You will find people interested in spiritual and/or religious subjects who post inspirational quotes, personal viewpoints, humor, art and graphics. Many of the posts are human interest pins that can lift your spirits and add a spiritual dimension to your day.

Here's How This Spiritual Practice Works:

If you haven't already, go ahead and sign up for a Pinterest account. It's free, and you can do it at Pinterest.com. Once you join, you can search for topics of interest to you, and find a multitude of pictures, quotes, posters, and information. Use these as stimulation for your spiritual enrichment, as you choose the ones that bring you meaning.

If you are so inclined, create a few boards that reflect your spiritual interests. There is excellent 'how-to' information on the site. As you surf the web, any time you find yourself captivated by an image, simply "pin it" to one of your boards. You are sharing your spiritual enrichment with others.

Consider Pinteresting as a spiritual practice. Become Pinterested in spiritual subjects. Contribute your own posts.

© 2014 Bil and Cher Holton, YourSpiritualPractice.com

Sacred Reading and Study

Make this spiritual practice a lifelong practice. Delving into spiritually-enriching materials will keep you on a growing edge that will deepen your spirituality and broaden your perspective in ways that you won't fully understand until you do it! We aren't just talking about the Bible here! Some of the most significant study areas we have found that deepen our spirituality are metaphysics, theosophy, anthroposophy, philosophy, quantum physics, the neurosciences, biology, epigenetics, and the social sciences. There is no shortage of material out there, so get busy and jump into a spiritual practice of sacred reading and study.

Here's How This Spiritual Practice Works:

Make it a habit to study spiritual material at least a half hour every day. Pick a spiritual subject that interests you. Expand your interests to topics that are thought-provoking and take you out of your comfort zone. There are a multitude of ways to accomplish this:
- Read a spiritually focused book;
- watch a spiritually rich YouTube, TED talk, DVD, or TV show;
- study a metaphysical text;
- delve into a metaphysical glossary;
- browse through a list of spiritual quotes.

If you are reading, highlight and/or underline sections that are especially meaningful. Write in the margins. Re-read exceptional passages. If you are watching something, keep your journal nearby, to capture insights and ideas.

Studying with an eye toward later practicing what you read will help you progress much faster than studying for inspiration only. What you put into practice will be a source of lasting spiritual growth. Keep records of your notes. Record your thoughts. Write original affirmations based on your reading.

© 1990, 2013 Bil and Cher Holton, YourSpiritualPractice.com

Eliminating Religious Relics

Religious relics are generally linked to limiting negative perspectives. They include such parochial antics as: dogma; supposed inerrant scriptural interpretations; close-minded literal translation biases; extreme judgmentalness; prejudicial exclusivity; the notion of an external, anthropomorphic goodie God in the sky; original sin; the Earth being created in six days; a red pajamaed, horned devil intent on welcoming us to hell; the sun standing still; etc.

Mainstream religious 'relics' are neurologically wired into the amygdala which produces our 'fight or flight' reactions. This inherited—and perpetuated—survival mechanism prevents many fundamental religious practitioners from experiencing more transcendent states of awareness which come from the neocortex area in our brain. The neocortex wiring is evolutionarily available too, it's just not the area of neural real estate fundamentalists (fundies) are as familiar with.

Here's How This Spiritual Practice Works:

As a spiritual practice, eliminating religious relics is a necessary condition if you want to grow spiritually. Hanging onto antiquated religious rules, assumptions, and 'walled' doctrines limit your spiritual growth and keep you stuck in the embedded theology of your youth. So, eliminating these 'relics' is a must.

Schedule time for self-reflection and assessment. Have a journal ready to record your insights and a-ha's. Move into a meditative state, asking yourself this question: What beliefs do I have that no longer match my current level of Consciousness?

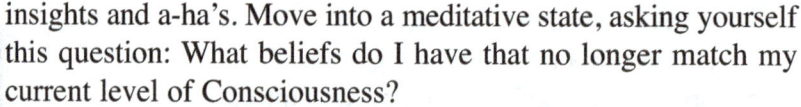

Capture the beliefs that pop into your mind, then reflect on each one, asking yourself if that belief is still serving you, or if it is creating unrealistic fears, doubts, or prejudicial behaviors. Question each belief, and as you feel ready, release the belief and identify the new belief you now have that replaces it.

This spiritual practice helps you monitor your progress, open-mindedness, and ability to let go of religious impediments. It is an excellent 'check up from the neck up' self-assessment. Whenever you find yourself slipping into a 'relic state-of-mind', remind yourself immediately that it is not part of your new belief system and level of Consciousness.

© 2014 Bil and Cher Holton, YourSpiritualPractice.com

Take a 'Self to Cell' Journey

You are composed of communes, colonies, cities,, and continents of trillions of cells in action. Your body is filled with cellular life. You are composed of hydrogen atoms and subatomic particles like quarks, leptons, and gluons that were present at the Big Bang. We're not kidding. Quantum physicists tell us that we are literally stardust as physical beings.

Subatomic parts of you are 15 billion years old. Other parts of you are a billionth of a second old. At a molecular and cellular level, you are a universe that is designed as a physical container for housing your particular level of consciousness and spirituality. And because you are a physical being, there is a constant need for healing and wholing the physical vehicle in which you find yourself.

The more you see healing as wholing from a spiritual perspective, the more you will come to know that your living cells contain more than biologists and geneticists are willing to admit.

You will see that to simply describe your network of cells as only biological containers comprised of a nucleus, membrane, receptors, tubes, fluid, and genetic markers is to miss the point of your biological footprint.

You will discover that your cells are highly intelligent beings with an innate divinity all their own. Written into the biography of your cells are the mysteries of life and consciousness, involution and evolution, time and space, the universe and the Multiverse!

In her book, *Secrets of Your Cells,* Sandra Barrett reminds us that "at every moment of every day, our cells orchestrate millions of molecular symphonies, guided by cellular intelligence in a delicately designed system of checks and balances, push and pull, collaboration and communication."

The sheer genius of the trillions of "molecular embraces" that are central to your biochemical functioning bridge both your biochemistry and your spirituality. Your cells are the biological expressions of your natural sacredness and spiritualness as a spiritual being having a human experience.

The extent of your spirituality and/or materiality influences each of your cell's life experience. Your cells respond to your thoughts, intentions, words, feelings, and actions. When you worry and are fearful, your internal pharmacy bombards your cells with stress hormones that, if activated too often, can harm your cells and move your entire being toward dis-ease. On the other hand, when you are joyful and loving, your cells are flooded with pleasure-inducing endorphins that elevate your immune system and fortify your cells, moving you toward wholeness.

Here's How This Spiritual Practice Works:

As a standard spiritual practice, take 'Self to Cell' journeys often. See your physical body as a cellular sanctuary. Imagine your cells working harmoniously together to ensure your complete healing and wholing. Envision your trillions of cells as tiny cauldrons of life-giving and life-sustaining energy.

Talk to your cells, thanking them for the incredible work they do. Ask forgiveness for anything you have done to bring injury or harm to them. Affirm their functioning with ease, blessing the work they do to team together for your highest health and wholeness.

Carl Sagan had no doubt as to your cells' superior resourcefulness and 'medical' knowledge. He reminds us that, "The blueprints, detailed instructions, and job orders for building you from scratch would fill about 1,000 encyclopedia volumes if written in English. Yet, every cell in your body has a set of these encyclopedias."

You have the pharmacy of pharmacies built into your DNA—and you have the intelligence of the universe distributed throughout your body within the diversity of the cells that constitute your bio-make-up. So, it just makes sense to communicate 'Self to Cell' in order to keep the wholeness that you are intact.

Partner with your cells. Maintain a loving, mutually-satisfying, symbiotic relationship. Cell-ebrate your cell power. Within your cellular genealogy is your wholing genie-ology! Experience the awesome wholeness and wholesomeness that come from the reciprocity between 'Self to Cell' and 'Cell to Self.'

© 2014 Bil and Cher Holton, YourSpiritualPractice.com

Life isn't about finding yourself.
Life is about creating yourself.
(George Bernard Shaw)

Silent Relaxation

For many of us, relaxation means zoning out in front of the TV at the end of a stressful day. But this does little to reduce the damaging effects of stress, nor does it contribute to your spiritual enrichment. To effectively combat stress and tap into your highest level of consciousness, you need to activate your body's natural relaxation response.

Silent relaxation is a spiritual practice that helps you to, well, relax! It helps you attain a state of increased calmness, comfort, and composure.

A technique growing in popularity is floatation therapy (developed by John Lilly in 1954), which uses a floatation tank and a solution of Epsom salt kept at skin temperature to provide effortless floating. But you don't need any special equipment to benefit from this practice. Research in the USA and Sweden has demonstrated that a powerful and profound relaxation experience can be attained in about twenty minutes ... just by setting the intention and doing it!

Here's How This Spiritual Practice Works:

There are a variety of ways to implement this spiritual practice. You may want to find a quiet place, lie back on a couch or bed, close your eyes, and take a cat nap. Use your smartphone alarm set to peaceful music as your "wake-up call."

There are also movement-based relaxation methods that incorporate light exercise such as walking, gardening, reading, reclining in a hammock, lounging in a gazebo, toe tensing, etc. These are considered movement-based relaxation methods because they involve eye movements, body motion, and/or outdoor sounds which can take your attention off of relaxing completely.

Toe tensing may seem like a bit of a contradiction to the previous relaxation methods, but by alternately tensing and relaxing your toes, you actually draw tension from the rest of the body. Try it!

- Lie on your back and close your eyes.
- Sense your toes by pulling all 10 toes back toward your face.
- Count to 10 slowly.
- Now relax your toes.
- Count to 10 slowly again.
- Now repeat the above cycle 5 times.

This spiritual practice is a good one to add to your spiritual resume on general principles. It's sort of like a portable Sabbath (resting from worldly concerns and material wants).

© 2008 Bil and Cher Holton, YourSpiritualPractice.com

Smartphoning

Smartphoning as a spiritual practice is "apps-olutely" one of the best ways to connect with almost anything you want to inspire your spiritual growth. We know, technology gets a bad rap these days—and it's true there is lots out there to distract us, waste our time, and create confusion in our consciousness. But smartphones can be used as a spiritual practice!

Here's How This Spiritual Practice Works:

There are: meditation apps, candle apps, singing bowl apps, yoga apps, soulcare apps, self-healing apps, soul journeys app, self-awareness apps, spiritual growth apps, spiritual disciplines apps, spiritual living apps, spiritual pathways apps, spiritual quotes apps, spiritual places apps, spiritual awakening apps, mindfulness apps, meditation timers and alarm clock apps, nature photo apps, Buddhist meditation apps, Buddhist mantra apps, world peace apps, prayer apps, plus hundreds, maybe thousands more to choose from.

You can email and/or text spiritual content to anyone, and receive emails and texts from anyone—anywhere in the world! Sending a riveting spiritual quote to a friend in need can turn his/her life around. Receiving a spiritually rich text can turn your day around, too!

Whether you plan on a spiritual pause for a couple of minutes or a longer reflective time of smartphone soul food, we know your "app-reciation" for the convenience of this spiritual practice will, no doubt, make it one of the basic tools in your spiritual toolkit. You can have spiritual experiences on the go or settle back on a cushion in your dedicated spiritual practice area and enjoy a spiritual moment.

© 2014 Bil and Cher Holton, YourSpiritualPractice.com

Create a Sound Byte Directory

This is your opportunity to capture powerful beliefs and perspectives that can become catalysts for your spiritual unfoldment. We invite you to make powerful quote collecting a regular practice. It'll keep you head and shoulders above negativity, inaction, and the stagnation that comes from a "flat-lined" ho hum existence.

Here's How This Spiritual Practice Works:

Collect positive, inspiring, motivational, and riveting quotes that deepen your spirituality, broaden your peacemaking and humanitarian perspectives, advocate health and wellness, enhance your connection with the Authentic You, and help you become a better person.

You can get "perspective-building" sound bytes on any topic from many sources. Google them. Find them in quotation books, self help books, leadership books, spiritual books, popular press science books, human potential books, DVD's, and CD's on any subject. You can be the beneficiary of a sound byte from something one of your friends says, or from a TV show or documentary, or from a conference you've attended, or from a tweet or text, or on Facebook, Pinterest, Instagram, etc.

Collect your sound bytes from A to Z in a file. Refer to them often. Post them on your web page so one pops up every time you open your website. Keep especially meaningful and inspiring bytes on your iphone and iPad, in your purse or wallet. Post them in your home and office. Refer to them when you've had a rough day or just want to be motivated. Come up with powerful sound bytes of your own.

This sound byte directory will be a perfect "partner" as you begin to adopt and adapt to its powerful influence on your unfolding Christ connection. It will help keep your consciousness elevated and centered on the positiveness, transcendentalness, and spirituality that bring happiness, inner peace, joy, and the confidence and perspective to become better aligned with your Higher Self, your Extraordinary Nature.

© 2000 Bil and Cher Holton, YourSpiritualPractice.com

T'ai Chi Movement

T'ai chi (T'ai chi ch'uan) is a Chinese 'hard-soft' martial art technique that not only improves your physical and emotional balance, but your spiritual balance (internal power) as well. As a spiritual practice, it focuses the mind solely on the slow movements of the martial arts forms it characterizes and helps to create a state of mental calm and clarity.

The slow, repetitive movements leverage each artful movement involved in the process so that your internal circulation is enhanced and your joints are relaxed and not strained. Since all human functions and processes follow the same laws as the Cosmos, it is to your benefit to flow with the Cosmos, instead of going against it. T'ai chi expresses that flow in its movements.

Here's How This Spiritual Practice Works:

Search out a beginning T'ai chi class in your local area, or go online and find an introductory T'ai Chi YouTube class, or a DVD you can purchase. Schedule a regular time each day to learn the basic movements of a T'ai Chi practice, and become aware of how interconnected your inner spirit is with your movements (once you learn them!).

Movement and stillness interact, and your movements are symbolized as Yin-Yang harmony which constitutes your inner well-being. In T'ai chi, you increase your energy level and enhance your energy flow through the movements. So, your pure energy rises to become 'heaven,' and your impure energy sinks to become 'earth,' opening your entire being to the spiritual joys of the Cosmos.

From a spiritual standpoint, the teachings of the Cosmos and the Limitless Void (God), together with the integration of spirit and energy, are the essences of the practice of Tai Chi. If practitioners do not understand these essences, they miss the deeper nature and benefits of T'ai chi as a spiritual practice.

© 2014 Bil and Cher Holton, YourSpiritualPractice.com

Resolute Thingumajiging

The spiritual practice of Resolute Thingumajiging means casting off a part of us that doesn't work anymore—things like lack of confidence, bad habits, debilitating addictions, recurring doubts, chronic fears, and negative attitudes—you know, things that minus you.

In Buddhist philosophy, ten general forms of afflictions are described: attachment, hostility, pride, ignorance, doubt, seeing the false 'I' as real, seeing the false 'I' as lasting or wrongly believing self to end with death, beliefs in wrong views, beliefs that certain behaviors lead to liberation, and wrong views in general.

In Christianity, the seven deadly sins, or cardinal sins, are considered to be our worst afflictions. They are: envy, gluttony, greed, lust, pride, sloth and wrath. Each is a form of idolatry-of-the-self (small 's' self, our egocentric self).

There's a story told about monkeys in the jungle who are captured by hunters who fill large, heavy jars with berries. When the monkeys reach in to grab the berries they get stuck because their clenched fist (full of berries) will not come out of the mouth of the jar.

The monkeys who are unwilling to let go of the berries are captured because they cannot carry the heavy jars. They are trapped by their own greed, gluttony, and stubbornness.

Although the story is probably apocryphal, it illustrates some important truths. People hang onto things (other people, ideas, beliefs, assumptions) that hold them hostage. We cannot walk the spiritual path unless we are willing to let go of material 'berries'—those "Thinumajigs" that keep us prisoner to our ego nature.

Here's How This Spiritual Practice Works:

It's as simple—and as difficult—as this: Let material "thingumajigs" go! Periodically take inventory and see what you are holding on to so tightly it is keeping you from the very things you are most desiring. Become aware of attitudes, beliefs, ideas, thoughts about yourself, habits, words you say, and every little "thingumajig" that separates you from the Truth of who you really are!

Make it a practice to release any and all "thingumajigs" that get in the way of your spiritual growth. Refuse to 'minus' yourself. See this spiritual practice as a sure route for traveling light so you can get to the Light inside of you!

© 2014 Bil and Cher Holton, YourSpiritualPractice.com

Honor Your BS

Before your lower jaw drops off—the 'BS' we're talking about stands for your 'Belief System.' After all, it's all BS, right? It's the story we tell ourselves to define our personal sense of 'reality.' Every human being has a belief system he/she lives by, and it's through this world view that we try to make sense of the world around us. We can even call our 'BS' the Theory of Everything (a quantum physics term that attempts to describe the nature of the universe).

There are generally two forms of belief systems that are seen as being at odds with each other: evidence-based versus faith-based. We want to add another option, science-based *and* faith-based, recognizing it is not "either-or" but rather "both-and." This spiritual practice is inviting you to honor both the science (evidence-based) and faith-based belief systems!

Science is used to building an evidence-based belief system, under the premise that the world is ultimately understandable through observation, experimentation, reliable replication, and prediction. The key element of science-based evidence is the recognition that we humans possess individual beliefs that make us capable of introducing bias into our interpretation of the world.

As a result, science attempts to mitigate against such subjective biases by demanding strict definitions of terms and conditions, as well as requiring that any evidence be capable of independent verification by others. This scientific method ensures that accepted results have been subjected to trials that may also be subject to bias. However, by requiring the strict adherence to procedure, such biases will cancel each other out and produce conclusions that are largely—hopefully—objective.

Faith-based belief systems are generally religious convictions that lack physical evidence. This is not to diminish their intrinsic value or suggest they are unfounded assertions, but rather to define an important difference between them and evidence-based beliefs. In short, a faith-based belief system is unequivocally based on the lack of supporting, observable evidence or evidence which may be impossible to collect.

Here's How This Spiritual Practice Works:

Regardless of what you individually believe, this spiritual practice calls for you to honor your current belief system, while at the same time remaining open to credible 'evidence' that surfaces which can refine and enhance your current belief system. It calls for you to create a credo of your BS (belief systems), and then set out to question it, stretch it, test it, expand it, and constantly enrich your awareness of the Truth of who you really are!

© 2015 Bil and Cher Holton, YourSpiritualPractice.com

Take 365 Vacations

Take 365 vacations this year! Wow! Is that a great benefit package or what? We're serious! Actually, let us be very specific here. Take 365 SPIRITUAL Vacations this year. Before you freak out and start telling us about your busy schedule, let's define what we mean by a spiritual vacation.

Here's How This Spiritual Practice Works:

A spiritual vacation is any specific amount of time in your day, from as little as 15 minutes all the way up to the entire day, where you intentionally choose to do some activity that is focused on your spiritual growth and enrichment. Let's give you some examples to illustrate how you could do this, depending on the amount of time you have.

Fifteen minutes to an hour: meditate; read a chapter in an inspirational book; listen to some spiritual music you enjoy; do some yoga exercises; pick a short spiritual practice from this book and do it; practice a mindful eating meditation.

Three hours: walk a labyrinth; take a class for your enrichment; go for a hike in nature; create a dreamscape collage; get a massage; focus on one of your seven Core Essences; contemplate on one of your 12 spiritual powers and choose an activity that strengthens it (The *Power Up Your Life* book we wrote is chock full of exercises to do that).

Full day: Go on a silent retreat; take a full-day class for your own spiritual enrichment; spend the entire day doing lots of little things that feed your soul; gather a group of like-minded friends and watch a movie, then interpret it metaphysically.

Part of the value of this specific strategy is to push you to try new things. For example, there are hundreds of types of meditation. You could take a month, and try a different type of meditation every day: a guided meditation; a Kundalini meditation; Following Your Breath meditation; eating meditation; walking meditation; drawing meditation; working meditation; sand mandala meditation; laughing meditation; singing meditation; scripture meditation ... the list goes on and on. This one spiritual practice could take you through half the year, easily!

Here's the deal: As you experience a new form of spiritual enrichment, you experience a shift in consciousness! You'll find it's not about taking enough time out of your day to "Be Spiritual." Instead, you'll discover that you're living your life AS Spirit!" Do you feel the difference? Spend more time as the Extraordinary You (your Higher Self) instead of the ordinary you. You will begin to experience what it means to make your life a spiritual practice.

© 1995, 2009 Bil and Cher Holton, YourSpiritualPractice.com

Volunteering

From very visible leadership to the quiet behind-the-scenes events, volunteer service allows people to meet others, deepen their connection to the community, and contribute to the greater good for all.

You are a unique spiritual being who has the capacity to give of your time, talents, and treasures—which are foundational pillars that ground you in this spiritual practice. When you mindfully give of yourself with a joyful heart, you grow spiritually and have opportunities to reveal your own authenticity and creativity in so many ways.

When you intentionally help others, you 'speak' a silent but visible appreciation for their worth and importance as human beings. One of the most beautiful compensations you'll find in this life is that you cannot help another without helping yourself.

One thing is for sure, many wonderful things won't ever be done unless you do them. What you do combined with your unique manner of sacred service cannot be accomplished by anyone else but you. Your particular way of volunteering is a gift that comes with your essence as a human being written all over it.

Your actions not only mold the present but shape the future. Your selfless acts of sacred service leave indelible imprints on the lives of those you serve, and are the touchstones of your own spiritual unfoldment.

Here's How This Spiritual Practice Works:

Determine what kind of volunteering is compatible with your skill sets and interests. Then build some form of volunteer work into your schedule. It can be daily, weekly, or monthly—the secret is to give back from your heart, with the intention of connecting with your Higher Self through the act of giving.

See sacred service as not only your way of giving back and paying it forward, but as connecting with others at a soul level.

© 2004, 2013 Bil and Cher Holton, YourSpiritualPractice.com

An In-Depth Reading: Work All Things Together For Good

A nine-year-old boy and a seven-year-old girl each want a juicy red delicious apple. Unfortunately, the apple of their eye is six feet above their heads, on the nearest low-hanging limb of a tree.

As they stand there looking at their dilemma, the little girl has an insight. She reminds her friend that all things are possible, and that they can divinely order their good. (She obviously had parents who were spiritual!)

Then she tells her friend that if she stands on his shoulders she can reach the lowest tree limb and grab couple of apples. He agrees, they take action, and pretty soon they each enjoy a delicious apple.

Spiritual principles work when we work them!

Here's another example we love. Dependng on your age, you may remember Jimmy Durante, a singer, comedian, and actor known for his big "schnozzel" and bigger heart. A story is told of a time when he and his agent were on their way to a radio show in Durante's honor. On the way, they made a quick stop at a veteran's hospital, because Jimmy had a soft spot for veterans injured in foreign wars.

Time was short, so Durante only did a portion of his one man show, singing, playing the piano, and tap dancing for the vets. As his agent began ushering Durante quickly toward the door after his performance, Jimmy stopped short as he noticed two veterans on the front row. They were wildly applauding his performance.

Now, fans showing their appreciation with applause was not unusual. What *was* unusual was that both of these veterans were amputees. One had lost his left arm and the other his right arm. But together they were able to applaud him using each other's good hand—and they were working together to show their appreciation with zeal! Jimmy was so overwhelmed with their appreciation that he returned to the stage and performed his entire show!

Talk about working all things together for good! Spiritual principles work when we work them!

These examples have one thing in common. They are all about the synergy of applying Truth principles, working things together for good.

In this spiritual practice, we're going to take a look at a commonly used phrase which reinforces the illusion of our separation from Spirit: "All things work together for good." (We hope you have already noticed, from our title, that we've made a little shift in wording which leads to a big shift in consciousness!) The traditional phrase, "All things work together for good," is based on a misinterpretation of Romans 8:28.

The scripture as it normally appears reads: "We know that for those who are called according to (God's) purpose, all things work together for good." (International Standard Version) The Lamsa Bible states it a little differently. It says, "We know that those who love God are helped by God in everything for good."

How many times have you heard someone say, "Things have a way of working out." or "It will turn out all right in the end because all things work together for good." Or, in its more extreme form, "God is good all the time."

Romans 8:28 does not say everything that happens is good. Nor does it say all things turn out like we want them to. It doesn't even say whatever happens to us is predestined.

We believe its truer meaning implies that Divine Presence underwrites all things for good, and that it is us who determines whether things work together for good or not. The good is there. We just need to express it—individually or collectively.

The phrase "to work together" comes from the root word *sunergeo*, which is Aramaic. It shares its origins with the Greek words *sunergiā*, which means "mutual cooperation," and *sunergos* which means, "working in concert."

The Apostle Paul used the word *sunergeo* in Romans 8:28 to explain the dynamic synergy which occurs in human, divine, and cosmic cooperation. At its most basic interpretation, the synergy of applying truth principles means "establishing unity, balance, and equilibrium between our consciousness and God Mind." It carries with it the idea that the whole is greater than the sum of its parts.

When we're attuned, when we're at-one-ment with Universal Principles, we can't help but to exclaim, "Yikes, this stuff works!"

The youngsters, in the opening story, used synergy to retrieve the apples. The veterans used their combined synergy to applaud Jimmy Durante. The words we used to describe this spiritual practice are synergized letters formed into words which are formed into sentences which we hope made sense.

We believe this is what Romans 8:28 is really telling us: When we synergize our human nature with our Christ Nature, we will be able to work all things together for good.

Notice we didn't say we will be able to work most things, or some things, or almost all things, or a few things together for good. **The principle is:** When you synergize your human nature with your Higher Self, your Christ Nature, the Extraordinary You—when you consistently make Divinely-guided choices, you *will* be able to work all things together for good.

Here's How This Spiritual Practice Works:

Use the following affirmation as a daily mantra: "I am working all things together for good."

© 2001, 2010 Bil and Cher Holton, YourSpiritualPractice.com

YouTubing

YouTubing is a virtual universe in itself. You can find any kind of spiritual and/or religious topic you want on YouTube, which is a video-sharing website. YouTubes range from twenty to thirty seconds to several hours of content that can keep you riveted to the spiritual and/or religious content you have chosen.

Here's How This Spiritual Practice Works:

Use your favorite search engine (we prefer Google), and type in YouTube followed by the topic you want to explore. You can find YouTubes with powerful inspirational music, meditations, talks on all subjects, humor, and just about anything else you want. You can download YouTubes as your favorites and archive them for later viewing. Because YouTubes are user-generated, our only caution is that while most of the content is credible and reliable, your discretion will be needed to ensure that you are watching plausible and valid content.

YouTubes can be a wonderfully enriching spiritual journey. Whether you view them in your home, office, or outdoors you can treat yourself to a 'tabernacle' experience using this amazing technology.

By the way, we invite you to check out our Global Center for Spiritual Practices YouTube channel: http://www.youtube.com/c/Yourspiritualpractice

We are continually adding new content, both our personal favorites and our own material, so feel free to subscribe!

© 2014 Bil and Cher Holton, YourSpiritualPractice.com

Yoga Practice

The practice of yoga is an art and science dedicated to creating union between your body, mind, and soul. It is a spiritual practice that assists practitioners in using their breath and body to foster an awareness of themselves as individualized beings intimately connected to the unified whole of creation. In short, it is about creating balance and equanimity in order to live in peace, good health, and harmony with the greater whole.

This art of creating union was perfected in India thousands of years ago and the foundations of yoga philosophy were written down in *The Yoga Sutra of Patanjali*,  approximately 200 C.E.. This sutra describes the inner workings of the mind and provides an eight-step blueprint for controlling its restlessness in order to enjoy lasting peace. Patanjali defined yoga as "the stilling of the changing states of the mind." Absolute freedom occurs when the lucidity of your material nature and spirit are in pure equilibrium and balance.

Here's How This Spiritual Practice Works:

The core of Patanjali's Yoga Sutra is this eight step yogic path. Upon practicing all eight steps (limbs) of the path, it becomes self-evident that no one element is elevated over another—even though they seem arranged in a hierarchical order. Each is part of a holistic focus which eventually brings wholeness and harmony to practitioners as they connect with their divine nature.

The eight steps (limbs) are as follows:
   Yama : Universal morality and ethics
   Niyama : Personal ethics and observances
   Asanas : Body postures
   Pranayama : Breathing exercises, and control of prana
   Pratyahara : Control of the physical senses
   Dharana : Concentration and cultivating inner perceptual awareness
   Dhyana : Devotion to your Divine Nature
   Samadhi : Union with your Divine Nature

The chief health benefits of a disciplined yoga practice are: stress relief, increased flexibility and muscular strength, weight loss, increase in over-all energy, improved sleep, over-all conditioning, and mind/body synchronization.

© 2002 Bil and Cher Holton, YourSpiritualPractice.com

About the Authors

Combine a flair for the dramatic, a deep understanding of metaphysics, an ability to think outside the box, and a knack for bringing scientific research and spiritual practices to life in practical ways, and you have defined the dynamic duo who co-authored this book. This exciting couple thrives on inviting people to walk the spiritual path on practical feet.

Revs. Bil and Cher Holton bring quite a background of business experience to their spiritual work. Together they founded The Holton Consulting Group, Inc. in 1982, and have worked with clients in the U.S., Canada, Germany, England, and South America, with a mission of leading, guiding, and inspiring people and organizations to live productively and joyfully at the speed of life ... one choice at a time.

As a subsidiary of their consulting firm, the Holtons created two publishing enterprises: Liberty Publishing Group (focusing on professional and personal publications) and Prosperity Publishing House (for spiritual material). They have published over 50 titles, including the highly acclaimed Metaphysical versions of Matthew, Mark, Luke, and John , and the Book of Revelation (the first ever verse-by-verse metaphysical interpretations of these New Testament books). They've also published metaphysical interpretations of the best-loved scriptures of the rest of the New Testament books in two volumes.

In 2005, the Holtons made the decision to follow their hearts, and entered into a spiritual training program that has led them to become ordained Unity ministers. After serving two different churches in North Carolina, they moved to a more global, catalytic role and co-founded The Global Center for Spiritual Practices, with a mission to guide and inspire people to walk the spiritual path on practical feet, by tapping into their Divine Nature.

On a personal note:

Bil and Cher take what they call "Indiana Jones Experiences" including white-water rafting, sky-diving, helicopter fly-bys and even fire walking to push their risk-taking envelopes. But one of their most exciting adventures led them into the world of ballroom dancing, and they are amateur student couple champions in several ballroom dance categories. They even have a ballroom dance floor in their home!

The Holtons have two sons, beautiful daughters-in-law, and four incredible grandchildren who live close to them, providing many opportunities for fun!

Life-Changing Spiritual Practices, Volume 1

A Sampling of Other Books by the Holtons:

By Rev. Dr. Bil Holton:
The Gospel of Matthew, New Metaphysical Version
The Gospel of Mark, New Metaphysical Version
The Gospel of Luke, New Metaphysical Version
The Gospel of John, New Metaphysical Version
The Book of Revelation, New Metaphysical Version
Get Over It! The Truth About What You Know That Just Ain't So! (co-authored with Paul Hasselbeck)
Get Over These, Too! More Truth About What You Know That Just Ain't So! (Co-authored with Paul Hasselbeck)

By Rev. Dr. Cher Holton:
Living at the Speed of Life: Staying in Control in a World Gone Bonkers!
PowerUP: The Twelve Powers Revisited as Accelerated Abilities (co-authored with Paul Hasselbeck)
Applying Heart-Centered Metaphysics: A Workbook to Bring Metaphysics To Life in Your Life (co-authored with Paul Hasselbeck)

Co-Authored by Revs. Drs. Bil & Cher Holton:
Power Up Your Life! Accessing Your Twelve Powers to Achieve Health, Happiness, Abundance, and Inner Peace
Spiritually Speaking: A Metaphysical Interpretation of Spiritual, Religious, and Modern Day Secular Terms ... for those who are more spiiritual than religious
Straight Talk About Spiritual Stuff
Reconciling the Church's Science Phobia: The Dance Between Science and Spirituality
The Manager's Short Course to a Long Career
Crackerjack Choices: 200 of the Best Choices You Will Ever Make
From Ballroom to Bottom Line ... in business and in life
Business Prayers for Millennium Managers
SUPPOSE . . . Questions to Turbo-Charge Your Business and Your Life

They also have many digital books available in a variety of formats through Smashwords.com/profile/view/bilholton

To order books or invite the Holtons to speak at your organization,
spiritual center, or association, contact them at:
cher@yourspiritualpractice.com

We invite you to visit their cutting-edge website, read their blog,
and sign up for their newsletter at:
www.YourSpiritualPracitice.com

ORDER FORM

YES! Please rush the following books to me! (Continue order on back)

Book Title   Quantity x Price per Book = Total Amount

_____   _____   _____   _____

_____   _____   _____   _____

_____   _____   _____   _____

_____   _____   _____   _____

_____   _____   _____   _____

Sub-total _____

Ordering a total of 5 or more books? You deserve a discount! Subtract 40% !! → Less Volume Discount _____

N.C. only – State Tax (7%) _____

Shipping/Handling Fee: $5.95 for up to 3 items; .99 each additional item (Media Mail. Call for rush orders.)

Shipping & Handling _____

TOTAL _____

We gladly accept all major credit cards, and checks make out to: Prosperity Publishing House

☐ Check   ☐ credit card _____ (Type)

Card Number _____

Exp. Date _____ Signature: _____

SHIP TO:

Name: _____

Address: _____

City/State/Zip: _____

Telephone Number: _____ Email: _____

May we add you to our mailing list?   ☐ yes please!   ☐ no thanks

www.ingramcontent.com/pod-product-compliance
Lightning Source LLC
Chambersburg PA
CBHW081119080526
44587CB00021B/3670